UP 'TIL NOW

UP 'TIL NOW

A MEMOIR

EUGENE McCARTHY

HARCOURT BRACE JOVANOVICH, PUBLISHERS

SAN DIEGO   NEW YORK   LONDON

Requests for permission to make copies of any part of
the work should be mailed to: Permissions, Harcourt
Brace Jovanovich, Publishers, Orlando, Florida 32887.

Robert Lowell's poem, "R.F.K.," which appears on
page 198 of this book, is quoted from his collection,
History, published in 1973 by Farrar Straus and
Giroux.

Library of Congress Cataloging-in-Publication Data

McCarthy, Eugene J., 1916–
    Up 'til now.

Includes index.
1. Democratic Party (U.S.), 2. United States—
Politics and government—1945– . I. Title.
JK2316.M3   1987   324.2736   86-14313
ISBN 0-15-193170-4

Designed by Julie Durrell

Printed in the United States of America

First edition

A B C D E

CONTENTS

FOREWORD

IF HISTORY is an interweaving of ideas with institutions that affect and are affected by persons, then this book is history. Certainly it is meant to be history, rather than a collection of reminiscences.

It covers a period of forty years, from the end of World War II to the year 1987—one-fifth of the time that the American Republic has been in existence. Its protagonists are three: the ideas of those years—the concepts that dominated government and politics—the politicians, and the institutions.

The dominating and influencing ideas of that forty-year period, which affected both foreign policy and domestic programs, were also three. The one affecting foreign and military policy most strongly was the idea—almost a doctrine—of the ideological distinction between the free world of democracies (some dictatorships) and the Communist world. This distinction was raised, principally, by Secretary of State John Foster Dulles to nearly a theological status. Dulles then proceeded to give his conception of world relationships, institutional strength, and support through treaties, compacts, and resolutions. Applying this distinction was relatively easy in Europe and in Asia, where it could be directed at historically existing Communist states—Russia in Europe, China in Asia. In the Western Hemisphere, the application was based on an ideological extension of the Monroe Doctrine. The extension went from the Doctrine's principle of forbidding foreign countries to try to dominate or control any nation in the Americas to the active campaign against anything that might be labeled a "foreign ideology."

The second idea, or complex of ideas, that affected domestic policy and domestic affairs primarily, but also had bearing on foreign affairs, was the new emphasis on human rights—equal rights, civil rights, i.e., human rights protected and promoted by civil power. Had the case for these rights not been made in the United States in the fifties and the sixties, the insistence on similar respect for the same rights by foreign countries (emphasized especially by the Carter administration and currently by the Reagan administration with more than necessary restraint relative to the South African policy of apartheid) would have been difficult, if at all possible.

The third idea, or set of ideas—almost an act of faith— was and is the disposition to look to procedures and reforms as a solution to almost every problem. This belief has been manifest especially in the seventies in drives to reform politics, to reform the courts, to reform the Congress, to reform the executive branch of the government, with Common Cause as the principal proponent of reform.

The institutions that the book reports on are the political parties, the presidency, the House of Representatives, and the Senate, as instruments, in some cases, of ideological forces standing against such ideological domination or influence.

Last, the book is about persons: presidents, like Harry Truman; members of Congress, like Speaker of the House Sam Rayburn, who believed in institutions, honored them, and strengthened them against attack by persons and ideas, and who were, in turn, strengthened in their offices by the institutions they understood, respected, and sustained. It is also about persons who surrendered to ideological pressure and raised the ideological banners against reason and restrained historical judgment. It is about persons who lacked understanding or respect for institutions, for their directing and stabilizing function in disordered times, and who, either for lack of understanding or by design, were willing to corrupt institutions for personal benefit or political advantage, both great and small.

PART I

POLITICAL INITIATION AND
THE RAYBURN YEARS

THEY ARE WRONG who think that politics is like an ocean voyage or a military campaign, something to be done with some particular end in view, something which leaves off as soon as that end is reached. It is not a public chore, to be got over with. It is a way of life. It is the life of a domesticated political and social creature who is born with a love for public life, with a desire for honor, with a feeling for his fellows; and it lasts as long as need be. . . .

It is not simply office-holding, not just keeping your place, not just raising your voice from the floor, not just ranting on the rostrum with speeches and motions; which is what many people think politics is; just as they think of course you are a philosopher if you sit in a chair and lecture, or if you are able to carry through a dispute over a book. The even and consistent, day in day out, work and practice of both politics and philosophy escape them. . . .

Politics and philosophy are alike. Socrates neither set out
benches for his students, nor sat on a platform, nor set hours
for his lectures. He was philosophizing all the time—while
he was joking, while he was drinking, while he was soldier-
ing, whenever he met you on the street, and at the end when
he was in prison and drinking the poison. He was the first
to show that all your life, all the time, in everything you do,
whatever you are doing, is the time for philosophy. And so
also it is of politics.

———Plutarch, *Moralia*

I did not know the Plutarch quotation when I first became
involved in politics, but as years of involvement passed I
came to think that if there were such a thing as a vocation
to politics, then Plutarch had defined it well. I did not come
from a political family. My direct involvement in politics
had been minimal until after I moved to the city of St. Paul,
Minnesota, to teach at St. Thomas College. The years immediately following the end of World War II were years of
political activity in Minnesota. The Democratic party and
the Farmer Labor party had become one party in 1944, in
large part because of the efforts of Hubert Humphrey. In
1947 a strong effort was being made to consolidate the party
and to give it new leadership, and incidentally to set the
stage for a race for the United States Senate, by Humphrey,
who was then the mayor of Minneapolis.

The initiative for political action on the St. Thomas campus and among the faculty came from a professor of history,
Marshall Smelser. He was interested both in the substance
of the politics of that year, and also, in a more detached way,

4

as history in the process. In 1947, under Smelser's urging, a number of St. Thomas faculty members attended precinct meetings and the county convention of the party. Faculty members were sustained by students, many of whom, in that year, were in school under the G.I. Bill of Rights, and old enough to vote. Smelser nominated me for county chairman, a nomination that did not carry. In 1948 Smelser left St. Paul for another teaching position, and I was left, more or less, to carry on the work he had initiated and sustained.

In 1948 I was elected chairman of the party for Ramsey County, made up primarily of the city of St. Paul.

In Ramsey County, as in contests for leadership throughout the state, two issues dominated. One was competence and the other was what was called "left wing" identification or association. There was a strong Trotskyite influence in some labor unions and farm radical groups, enough to justify our claim that we would eliminate any such forces from positions of power in the party.

In early summer of 1948 I decided to run for Congress against an incumbent Republican. Although my running for Congress was not a fulfillment of long held hopes and careful planning, it did seem at the time, as it does in retrospect, to have been an orderly progression from study and reflection on political and social problems and thought. With my announcement of my intention to run for Congress, the unity of support that I had had in the contest for the chairmanship of the party in the county quickly dissipated. New was set against old. Regulars against irregulars.

The regulars of the Democratic Farmer Labor party were regular in the traditional party way. They controlled city government. The mayor, when I first became involved in St.

Paul politics, was John McDonough. John was suffering at
the time from the results of a stroke of some consequence
and seriousness. His speech was impaired, slowed down
principally, as was his physical mobility. He walked not
with a shuffle, but more like a bishop in a religious proces-
sion, one carrying a reliquary or a religious symbol. His
movement was careful, measured, seemingly reverential.
His face, following the stroke, was fixed in a kind of beatific
smile, the same whether he was attending a baseball game,
a political rally, or a religious service. His greeting and farewell was a "God bless you."

John usually moved surrounded or accompanied, as a
bishop might be, by secular deacons and subdeacons. His
city council, made up of commissioners, were cast in the
Chicago and Tammany mold. The strong man of the council
when he was in office was John Findlan, known as Big John,
commissioner of finance. His assistant was Paddy McDer-
mott. Out of office, Big John and Paddy returned to their
work on the railroad, John as an engineer and Paddy as his
fireman. A second commissioner of note was Jack Barfuss,
who had the concession of city garbage, which he fed to pigs
on his farm across the Mississippi from the city. The Italians
of the city were represented by Frank Marzitelli; the Jewish
community, for a time at least, by Milton Rosen, suspected
of being a Republican. Republicans in desperation had taken
to running fallen-away Irish Democrats for city offices, but
with little success.

The spokesmen for the black population were generally
ministers, with the exception of "Good Daddy" Hall.

Good Daddy ran a kind of after-hours club for his black
constituency, providing essentially the same services—

after-hours drinking, a little gambling (cards and crap shooting), and so on—given to high white citizens of the city by the Minnesota Club, the Athletic Club, and several other clubs less well known.

When to my surprise he rose to second my nomination as a candidate for Congress, I asked a local politician of some experience who he was. He told me, adding that Good Daddy had been arrested some twenty to thirty times. His nominating speech was so good that when because of parliamentary complications I had to be renominated I asked him to speak again. He did.

The story of Good Daddy as a force in St. Paul ended years later when, again arrested, he was given the choice of six months in the workhouse or exile. He accepted exile, and in the bus station gave a farewell address in which he recounted the good things that had marked his life in St. Paul and observed that all were now gone, or was, referring to himself, about to leave without regret. The bus which was scheduled to arrive just as he ended his speech was late. Good Daddy slumped and was silent. The last words spoken of him and to him in St. Paul were by his niece, Sybyl, who had come for him from Waterloo, Iowa. Sybyl said, "Pick up your suitcase, Ada, here comes the bus." We finally knew his name.

The labor leaders of that time were also of classical mold. They were men risen from the ranks, but existing in the afterglow of men of thought like Phil Murray of the steelworkers and Bill Green of the American Federation of Labor. They were men who had suffered physical violence in the cause of labor during the thirties and had worked to organize labor without the help and protection of Federal legislation.

Take Frank Thill of the plasterers union; in moments of excitement he would declare that the time had come "to deal the cards under the table," words that ranked closely with those of the head of the building trades in Minneapolis, who under charges of corruption asserted that he had little morality, but a hell of a lot of ethics.

There was order in the structure of union politics. Carpenters and milk drivers, as should have been expected, were generally Scandinavian. Metal workers, led by Mike Schmitt, were Germans. In the steelworkers, actually the iron mine workers, of Northern Minnesota, the Yugoslav force was recognized—persons like Smilovich and Crumpetich. The Poles were the machinists, and so forth.

City Hall retainers, guards, and general service employees seemed to run to former boxers, and especially to former sparring partners. St. Paul was then in the twilight of its great boxing era. Tommy Gibbons, who had fought Dempsey for fifteen rounds in Shelby, Montana, was sheriff of Ramsey County. In charge of keeping the courthouse brass well polished was "Honey Boy" Jackson of sparring partner fame, who gave, when he decided to run for city office, his full name—Toussaint L'Ouverture Jackson.

My campaign became a kind of school project, or rather, a schools' project. The core of my campaign effort were the faculty and student body of St. Thomas College, supported by faculty members and students of other colleges and universities in St. Paul. Hamline, a Methodist university, pitched in. Some of the student support was based on political belief, especially among the G.I. students. Others joined out of school spirit, or academic identity. Some (freshmen, I suspect) were impressed into distributing campaign publications by upperclassmen. I was opposed in the primary by an American Federation of Labor endorsed candidate. The union of the American Federation of Labor and the Congress of Industrial Organizations had not yet taken place. The CIO and the auto workers supported me as the party-endorsed candidate. The AFL, however, properly stated that their organization was the core of the party, at least in local politics. (The Democrats had elected a congressman—only one for a single term—in all the years since World War I.) Curiously, the basis upon which the AFL made its claim was little different from that stated by the labor leaders in their early announcement that they had a special right and claim to pick the candidate of the Democratic party in the presidential race of 1984.

My margin of victory in the primary was approximately five hundred votes. In the general election, supported by the party and by the labor movement, victory was clear. But what was most surprising to me was the depth of loyalty that can develop in a campaign. Loyalty that is complete, deep, and lasting.

The support I received in the anti-Vietnam campaign of 1968 was described by some observers as motley and unprecedented. It was in fact little different from that which I had received in 1948—from students, some old enough to vote, some not, old liberals, and party persons, especially women. Margaret Moore, a policewoman, showed up at meetings with a shopping bag full of favors she had picked up on her beat, rulers, ashtrays, etc., to be given out to party workers. Mrs. Jasper Russel, in a grand McArthurlike gesture, nominated herself for state chairwoman with an opening declaration that after all her years of service to the party she should not have to nominate herself, but that since no one else had done so, or would do so, she was doing it herself. Women like Irene Maloney and Agnes Malone, and nuns just beginning to become involved in politics, were joining out of loyalty to the Irish. And there were persons like Ray Devine of the stationary engineers; John Ohara, ex-boxer, primarily a sparring partner for better known and more successful St. Paul fighters, and a member of the bartenders union. We were scarcely financed in the primary, our expenditures coming to a little more than $4000, and we were underfinanced in the general election.

Victory in that election was more than personal. It was a party victory. President Truman in his campaign had made the record of the Eightieth Congress the issue, setting against its record of position and obstructionism, a challenging program. As distinguished from its approach to some campaigns, especially recent ones, the Democratic party in 1948 had a platform before it had candidates, both congressional and presidential. The first commitment of all was to the platform, which included as central issues civil rights and the Marshall Plan. Congressional candidates, many of whom had won by a larger percentage of the vote than had President Truman, shared the satisfaction and the elation of his come-from-behind victory, and came into the Eighty-first Congress with enthusiasm and hope. It was all just a little short of the attitude reflected in the title Dean Acheson gave to his book on post–World War II policy and diplomacy, *Present at the Creation.*

The Democratic leadership in the Congress greeted the newly elected congressmen gladly. Frustrated by the preceding Congress, and fearing that their leadership positions would be in jeopardy in the elections of 1948, they now found themselves back in power with a working majority. The majority had been elected, save for the southern congressmen who were opposed to civil rights legislation, on a commonly held platform. The former leaders—Sam Rayburn as Speaker and John McCormick as majority leader— were resettled in their offices. Since the seniority system was as yet unchallenged, committee chairmanships and appointments went largely according to formula. Sam Rayburn was the dominant and controlling force, and the House of Representatives, until after his death in the early 1960s, operated according to his conception of that branch of government and his conception of what the Constitutional role of the Speaker of the House of Representatives was.

Even during the Eisenhower presidency, when the Democratic party was casting about for a spokesman, Rayburn, unlike subsequent speakers, refused to be cast as the head of the Democratic party, even as a titular head. He left the role to other party officials, both in and out of Congress— Adlai Stevenson, after defeat, and in a limited way Lyndon Johnson, when Lyndon became majority leader of the Democrats in the Senate. Rayburn seldom left the Speaker's chair to address the House of Representatives, and then only when he thought the matter under debate was compelling in importance, or when he thought that the House of Representatives was about to do something that would be foolish and reflect on the integrity of that body.

He was so true to the rules of the House and to its traditions that members could never accuse him of unfairness or partisanship. Republican Congressmen Joe Martin of Massachusetts and Charlie Halleck of Indiana, the leaders of the opposition party for a good part of Rayburn's tenure as Speaker, were left in a frustration of respect.

"Those that go along, get along," was one of his favorite expressions. It was a good working rule with him as Speaker. With other Speakers or leaders, it might well have been questioned.

Sam believed that the House of Representatives needed rules, even an occasional rule change, but he also believed that under ordinary conditions the business of the House could be accomplished through accommodation and trust among members and between the leaders of the two parties. He was against sweeping reorganizations. When commenting on the Reorganization Act of 1945, which had done little to disturb the traditional lines of authority and responsibility some five years after it was adopted, he observed that the only good in it was that it provided an increase in salaries and a retirement program for members of Congress. What he would have said about the great reorganization of the early seventies would probably have been unprintable.

Although newly elected members of the Eighty-first Congress were somewhat restless under the established order and talked of challenging both the seniority and the committee systems, most became reconciled to it and found sufficient satisfaction in the legislative progress that occurred in that and subsequent Congresses. Those who were reelected began to see prospects of their own achievement of seniority and of the advantages that would go with that status. I began writing an article on the evils of the system in my first term, but before I finished it, or found a publisher (I forget which), I abandoned the effort, reassured by recollection of a statement by Gilbert K. Chesterton. When commenting on the medieval and earlier practice of having the eldest son or daughter of a king succeed to the throne on the death of a monarch, Chesterton pointed out that, whereas the practice was illogical and often resulted in the seating of bad or inadequate rulers, over the years it seemed to work out, and that, in any case, it did seem to save a lot of trouble.

There was structure and hierarchy in the Rayburn House of Representatives. The lines of authority, power, and responsibility within the House were clear, as were the distinctions in role between the House and the Senate, the courts, and the executive branch of the government.

Sam is reported to have leaned down from his Speaker's chair in the House chamber just before or after President Truman gave his first State of the Union Address and said, "Remember Harry, you are also still Harry Truman."

The sense of idealism, of good things to come through legislative action—even a kind of new-member euphoria in that first Congress for me and for many liberal, relatively young Democrats—was interrupted early by political reality. One of these realities was a proposal to significantly increase veterans benefits, pensions, etc., far beyond the G.I. Bill. The author and principal sponsor was John Rankin of Mississippi, supported by his Veterans Committee. Many of John Rankin's actions in Congress were a mixture of idealism, or principle, and mischievous challenge to the leadership. He was not only an outspoken opponent of civil rights legislation and pro-Israel policies, but came very close to being racist and anti-Semitic. His Veterans bill was a challenge to both the Truman administration and the leadership of the Democratic party in Congress. Ironically, he was able to bring up the bill and circumvent the Rules Committee by using an old rule, seldom if ever used in the twentieth century. It was a rule adopted in the post–Civil War days to prevent Southern congressmen from obstructing proposals to provide pensions for soldiers who had fought on the Union side. Nearly one hundred years later that committed Southerner turned to this ancient rule. World War II veterans in the Congress, most of them there in their first terms, were called upon to make the fight against the Rankin proposal. They did, being joined at a critical point by John Kennedy, who spoke out strongly and passionately against the measure. Despite these efforts, at the end of the general roll call the measure had prevailed by a few votes.

The leadership, principally Speaker Rayburn, then called on older members to show courage. Under the rules of the time, members could change their votes up to the time the vote was finally announced. The Democratic delegation from Philadelphia was Rayburn's principal target, and he meant to make it his reserve force. It was a noteworthy bunch, consisting of four members, Green, Granaham, Barrett, and Chudoff. They were all of the same height, roughly five feet four inches. The word was that Bill Green, who was the political boss of Philadelphia, would not approve any Democratic candidate for Congress who was taller than he. None of the delegation was. Moreover, the delegation of four customarily sat in the last row in the House chamber and voted as one man.

The procedure for changing one's vote at the time was very public. It required that the member seeking to make the change walk down into the well of the House, be asked how he had voted, and then announce his change in position, often to the jeers of members of the House who favored his first position. In this case, the word went out to the Philadelphians, who, in line, following their leader—Congressman Green—proceeded down the aisle all the way from the back of the chamber, changed their votes, and thus marginally defeated the Veterans Bill. They looked like men walking the plank to certain defeat in the next election. All survived, as did John Kennedy.

Among the better known and singular, if not distinguished, Democratic delegations in the House of Representatives in addition to the Philadelphia quartet were the Texas delegation, the New York delegation, and the Illinois delegation—more specifically, the Chicago delegation. Not all members of these delegations would have been given the "Good-House of Representatives-Keeping Seal of Approval," and they might well have fallen out with Common Cause had that organization been in existence monitoring the Congress in those years. On the other hand, the legislative achievements accomplished with the support of these delegations in the fifties and sixties serve as historic support of the poet William Stafford's warning, "If you purify the pond, the water lillies die."

The New York delegation made up the major part of the so-called Tuesday-to-Thursday Club, the members of which arrived for congressional sessions on Tuesday mornings and returned to New York on Thursday evenings. As a rule, they spent three nights a week in Washington, a reality noted by Congressman Delaney of New York when he told of his three friends in Washington who ran bum restaurants; his only choice was to decide the order of the three for his weekly three nights of dining out.

The core of the New York delegation was Irish: Delaney,

Keogh, Rooney, Donald O'Toole, Charlie Buckley. But there was a comparable contingent of Jewish members, headed by Manny Celler, the chairman of the House Judiciary Committee, which spearheaded the civil rights battles. Adam Clayton Powell was there as well, along with an Italian quota.

The Chicago delegation was, if anything, ethnically more in balance than the New York City delegation. It had, one assumes, almost in direct proportion to their constituencies in Chicago, Irish, Jewish, Black, Polish, and Italian members. But the lead man was Tom O'Brien.

This acknowledged leader had been at various times Sheriff of Cook County. The disrespectful called him "Blind Tom," while the respectful referred to him as "The Sheriff." Tom regularly wore a grey or blue suit and, when out of doors, a grey fedora. In winter he wore a great black coat with a velvet collar. In public he was always accompanied by an aide he called simply "Johnny." Johnny dressed like Tom, and usually walked not with Tom, but a few steps behind him, a position possibly carried over from the days when Johnny had been secretary to Tom the Sheriff. Tom seldom spoke in Congress. One day he startled the House of Representatives as a procedural issue was raised by shouting, "I object!" Experienced members said that it was possibly the longest speech Tom had given in his whole congressional career.

I suggested to Tom one day that he should write a book based on his experiences called "The Lesser of Two Evils." "Boy," he said, "If I had to face only the lesser of two evils, it would have been easy. Usually the choice was among more than two." He told me of one of his hardest choices;

one he had to make upon becoming sheriff. The three great evils, as Tom saw them, were gambling, illegal liquor, and prostitution. "I knew that you can't take everything away from the people," said Tom, "and decided that I would leave them gambling and liquor, and concentrate on suppressing prostitution," a decision that may have reflected Tom's Irish puritanism, or Jansenism. In any case, it was a difficult undertaking, according to Tom. If any "house" had as much as fifteen minutes warning, a warning likely to come through law enforcement channels, according to Tom, there would be no basis for arrests. The only thing that worked was for him, accompanied by his reluctant aide, Johnny, to go to a house and ask the madam to let them see the girls, at which point he would direct Johnny to call the closest police or sheriff's office to advise the law enforcement officers that the sheriff was waiting, at the address given, for the expected raid. Then meditatively, Tom would say, "I haven't had it easy."

In addition to the Rayburn strength—the Philadelphia, New York, and Chicago delegations—there was that of the Texas delegation, with many members in key positions: Paul Kilday, Albert Thomas, Wright Patman, Homer Thornberry, and others. Clarence Cannon of Missouri, parliamentarian, military expert, and defender of the constitutional rights of the House of Representatives, was Rayburn's chief lieutenant. He was the chairman of the House Appropriations Committee during most of the years that Sam Rayburn was Speaker of the House and was probably the closest to being a genius of any member of the Congress that I met in the twenty-two years that I served in Congress. His genius was manifest especially in his knowledge of the rules of the

House, his codification of them, his handling of appropriation bills, and his knowledge of what was in them.

In 1950, Congressman Cannon, hoping to get better control of government finances, was moved to handle the expenditures of the federal government in a consolidated appropriation bill. Social Security expenditures at that time were considered to be outside the general budget, which at that time came to about $50 billion dollars. After a year's experiment with the consolidated appropriation, Chairman Cannon determined that it was a less effective procedure than the traditional one of dealing with the federal budget department by department, and consequently returned the House of Representatives to the earlier practice. In 1986 the total federal budget was in excess of $900 billion, and lesser men than Cannon will attempt to deal with it following a procedure that was tried and found wanting over thirty years ago—a reminder of the consequences of having decisions made by those marked, as Yeats said, by "unremembering hearts and heads."

Chairman Cannon believed in having strong lieutenants and trusting a limited number—approximately five subcommittee chairmen, according to the Caesarian theory of delegating authority. The big five in the Cannon table of organization were Albert Thomas of Texas, chairman of the Independent Offices Appropriations Committee, John Fogarty of Rhode Island, chairman of the Health, Education, and Welfare Appropriations Committee, John Rooney of New York, chairman of the Appropriations Committee for the State Department, Dan Flood of Pennsylvania, chairman of the Armed Services Appropriations Committee, Mike Kirwan of Ohio, chairman of the Public Works Appropriations Committee. These were the big spenders—or if not big by contemporary standards, the important spenders. Each of the chairmen was considered eccentric in some way, distinguished and competent in his field, fair and responsible. The latter characteristics were accepted as justifying some eccentricity and an occasional excess.

Albert Thomas ran his committee, a very complicated one because of the range of its jurisdiction, like a ringmaster in a circus—a three-ring one, at least. Members of the House who had nothing before the committee would occasionally drop in just to see the proceedings, or, as some called them, the "shows." One member charged Thomas with having waxed the witness chair so that anyone who appeared before him could remain seated for only a few minutes and then slip off with the chairman's blessings.

John Fogarty of Rhode Island was chairman of the Health, Education, and Welfare Appropriations Committee during the years in which the fields of his committee's responsibility were greatly expanded, especially those of health, hospitalization, and medical research. It was during these years that medical science made great leaps forward. The leaps forward were not altogether a blessing to people like Fogarty who stood at the switches. False hopes were stirred. Questionable research was approved. Hospitals were built, or overbuilt. The pressure was on for almost unlimited expenditures. I recall spokespersons for the National Institute of Health asking members of Congress privately not to provide more money for cancer research, because there were not enough deserving projects.

The most successful lobbyist for expanded medical research and services was Mary Lasker of New York. She

parlayed campaign contributions into friendship, and attention to members of Congress, especially in the Senate, into
a major expansion of all medical services and study. Senator
Lister Hill of Alabama (named, one must assume, after Lister
the bacteriologist) was her special representative, to the
point that one year, while asking for support for his proposed appropriations, Fogarty said, "Let me outdo Lister and
the Senate, this one year." He got what he asked for, but was
outbid by the Senate. He was heard, either speaking for
himself or quoting someone else, saying that the Senate (at
that time averaging considerably above the House of Representatives in age) would appropriate unlimited funds for
any care or research related to the diseases and disabilities
of aging males.

Fogarty's main interest after health—possibly before it—
was a United Ireland. For one night he enjoyed the satisfaction of knowing that the House of Representatives had cut
off all aid to England (this in the immediate post–World War
II years when the aid was significant). It was restored the
next day.

John Rooney represented a Brooklyn district in the Congress. Brooklyn is not, or was not in the fifties and sixties,
particularly internationalist. John, as chairman of appropriations for the State Department and its programs, was a hard
taskmaster when witnesses from the State Department appeared before his committee. Some dreaded appearing before him. Others got used to him and even came to like him,
as prisoners are reputed to respond under some circumstances to their captors or guards. Despite the chairman's
attitudes, methods, and reputation for being tight fisted, it
was through his committee that money was approved for

the support of the expanded foreign aid programs that followed World War II.

Rooney's reputation for being thorough and demanding in his examination of witnesses and programs left potential critics and opponents of aid programs, as well as of foreign aid policies, at a disadvantage in opposing such policies and programs. An annual event in each session of Congress, almost a ritual, was the challenge to Rooney's appropriations by the ranking Republican on the committee, one Frank Keefe, from Wisconsin. Rooney was scarcely five feet tall. Keefe was an imposing six feet three or four. His face was typical of a certain type of Irishman, with a great hawk nose and beetling eyebrows. When the word spread that the confrontation was about to take place, House members gathered in great numbers for the action, which usually began with Keefe making reference to Rooney as the former assistant district attorney from Brooklyn, and Rooney returning the questionable compliment by referring to Keefe as the former "county attorney" from Oshkosh.

Then the battle was joined by Chairman Cannon, standing with a half smile on his face (as much a sign as he ever gave of inner feelings) as his lieutenant Rooney carried the field. Occasionally a State Department spokesman might win a point off of Rooney, that is if money was not involved. The director of Foreign Service personnel did so when under questioning about the fact that before a Foreign Service officer was assigned or promoted, reports were requested as to the qualifications of his wife. (The question of reports on husbands of women in the Foreign Service was not raised.) In any case, the State Department official acknowledged that such reports were solicited and made part of the file, and admitted that he had read many of them, and he had come to the conclusion that all Foreign Service officers were married to the same woman—one who possessed all virtues: intelligence, grace, dedication to the Foreign Service, loyalty to the country, beauty, family concern, and so on.

The chairman of the Public Works Appropriations Committee was Michael Kirwan, generally referred to as "Iron Mike" because he never smiled and laughed only silently. He was also known as "You-see-what-I-mean Kirwan," because that phrase occurred before, after, or as an interruption of every remark he made. Mike had come up the hard way and was quick to point (for it showed clearly) to the bump on his head where he had been struck by a foreman as he worked sorting coal as a boy of fourteen. Mike had little love for corporate or company officials of any kind. Handling appropriations for Public Works was a mean test, for it was in his committee that the real pressures for "pork barrel" projects came to bear. Getting approval for locks, dams, and reclamation projects was not easy. Getting the money to finance the projects was, and is, another matter. Critical in the early stages of most such projects is the support of the Army Corps of Engineers and getting at least a slightly positive benefit-over-cost ratio.

The Corps is one of the great military/political complexes in history. Originally set up in 1802 to direct military construction and engineering, it was later given jurisdiction over navigational construction not only on the seacoast but also over inland waterways. Jurisdiction over flood control and inland navigation gave the Corps new influence and power, as well as personnel and opportunity for careers and promotions within the Army far beyond what would have been possible had the Corps' activities been limited to military construction. The power of the Corps to approve internal projects gave it great political influence with the Congress, and reciprocal congressional support as well. Although the Corps was slow to shift to environmental engineering, there were signs of interest and response during the Kirwan days indicating that the Corps was ready to extend its role of "lowering the hills, raising the valleys" as Scripture had it, to that of deepening the rivers, controlling the floods, and of generally "making straight the way of the Lord."

There at the crossroads, the gates, the turnstile, and the floodgates stood Iron Mike. He was a fair man, possibly a little partial to those to whom he referred out of the side of his mouth as "one of us." There were degrees of belonging to this category, not unlike the degree and order of the choirs of angels, which range from simple angels to the seraphim. To be fully included in Mike's "one of us," a person had to be a liberal Democrat, pro-union, anti-corporate power, Irish, for a United Ireland, and Catholic.

There was some good in each project approved by Kirwan's committee; if not economic or environmental good, certainly political. He sought little for his own district beyond a canal from Lake Erie to Youngstown, Ohio, the home of the Youngstown Sheet and Tube Steel Mill. The canal was to be called the Kirwan Canal. The sheet and tube company has closed its steel mills in Youngstown. Mike did not live to see the closing. His most noted failure was his continuing effort to establish an aquarium in Washington. Occasionally he would get approval in the House of Representatives, or near approval, but concurrence in the Senate never followed. He liked to watch fish, Mike said, because they were quiet and peaceful as a rule. He thought their influence would be good in the city of Washington. The one project on which he drew the red line, year after year, was the Tom Bigbee Warrior River Project, which survived his death and was finally approved in 1980 when Howard Baker of Tennessee was majority leader of the Senate. The period of gestation, which sometimes accelerated, sometimes slowed—if not stopped altogether, covered nearly forty years.

Every year that I was in the House of Representatives, at the time when public works were under consideration, there was an almost ritualistic presentation of the project by John Rankin of Mississippi; following that, there was a ritualistic rejection, usually led by Representative John Taber, a New York Republican. Rankin led off with a description of the potential of the project—a slack water route at worst and an affirmative current at best—a water route all the way from Cairo, Illinois, down the Mississippi to New Orleans, and from there in coastal waters to Mobile, Alabama. From Alabama it went north with the help of the Tom Bigbee project to connect with the Tennessee River, and then on down that river to Cairo to complete the circuit.

John Rankin was a small man and an excitable one. As he got into his speech in support of the Tom Bigbee, his face gradually turned a brilliant red and his voice rose higher. By the time he had finished, Taber was ready. Taber was a large man with a deep voice. Those who sat near him during the Rankin speeches said that about halfway through he'd begin to rumble like a restless volcano or a rockslide beginning to move. As Taber proceeded into speech, declaring the Tom Bigbee to be the worst public project ever conceived by man and describing the river as approximately six feet wide and six inches deep in high-water periods and running through solid rock for two hundred miles, his voice would grow deeper and deeper and his face would pass from blood red to deep purple. After he finished, his last syllables would reverberate through the House chamber. One member of the House, suffering from deafness, was reported to have leaped from his seat in the House when John hit one of his lowest tones, declaring that he could hear, in the manner not unlike the blind man of scriptural note.

My first experience with Chairman Kirwan came early in my congressional career. I assume that because of my academic background, and possibly out of desperation, a spokesman for the Library of Congress approached me to ask for my help in trying to get Kirwan to approve a modest appropriation for the library. It was not for new books or shelves or equipment to service scholarly pursuits. Rather, it was a request for money to install more toilet facilities in the library. According to my library informants, the number of toilet units of the various kinds, was not (relative to the potential users) "per capita," or whatever anatomical measure one might use to determine this kind of need adequate. Mike was unmoved by my appeal for action to relieve the stress of scholars and library visitors. He did come up to me after I had finished speaking, and, talking behind his hand as was his habit, advised me that he was not fixed in his opposition to the additional facilities, but was waiting for the library's response to his request that it hire a couple of guards or attendants. I left this information with friends of the library.

Minnesota was not a state in great need of major public

works. Neither the geology, geography, or industry of the state were such that they could be well served by public works—except, that is, for the nine-foot channel Mississippi project that had been completed as far as St. Paul in the thirties. We Minnesotans, as members of Congress, lent support to the St. Lawrence Seaway, with Duluth harbor as its midcontinental terminus. But the St. Lawrence was more than a Minnesota project. It was something that had to be done, if for no other reason than that it could be done. And so it was. There was some talk of Duluth becoming a great port for transatlantic shipping, in somewhat the same spirit that Duluth had been talked about at the beginning of the twentieth century as the "New Chicago." Those who read omens were discouraged at the celebration of the completion of the seaway in Duluth, when Hugh O'Brien, then starring in a western series on television, was brought in to ride a horse up the gangplank and onto the first freighter in port —a symbolic uniting of West and East and beyond that, between us, Europe, and the rest of the world. To the chagrin of O'Brien and the distress of the promoters of the day, the horse refused to do his part.

The state did have one public works project singularly its own. That was the construction of what was described as the "upper lock and dam" of the Mississippi between St. Paul and Minneapolis. This lock and dam was the last work in the nine-foot channel Mississippi project. It was designed to get barges and boats over St. Anthony's Falls, and so to service Minneapolis. The lower lock and dam had been completed before World War II. It provided a lift only halfway up the falls. The war interrupted building plans, and some ten years later, after industrial development in Minneapolis had shifted away from the river and other changes in river use had taken place, the state and the Corps of Engineers was left with a lock and dam capable of lifting boats and barges halfway up St. Anthony's Falls. The completion of the project was approved and accomplished. Unfortunately, the week before the dedication, *Look* magazine, in listing the five worst public works projects of the year, included the upper lock and dam. Although I represented the city of St. Paul as a major part of my constituency, and St. Paul had had little interest in opening the river to Minneapolis, I was asked to speak at the ceremony. For some reason, neither of the United States senators nor the congressmen appeared for the dedication. The best I could do was speak of this as the fulfillment of a dream that must have gone back to missionary explorers—like Hennepin and Marquette, both of whom have streets named after them in Minneapolis, and of Nicollet, a nonmissionary explorer whose name was carried on a street, a bank, and a hotel.

My only real success with a public works project came quite by accident. Barge operators, largely shippers of grain on the Mississippi, regularly complained about the problem of the old lock and dam at Keokuk, Iowa. The locks there were so small that barge tows had to be broken up and passed through in segments. One year as the appropriations for public works bills were about to come up for debate, I decided to make a kind of negative case for Keokuk Dam, and to establish at least a marginal reputation as an economizer. (Even though in the twenty-two years that I was in Congress the national debt increased by less than it will increase in one year of the Reagan administration, other liberals and I were continuously under attack as big spenders and as fiscally irresponsible.) In any case, our strategy was to examine the appropriations bill and pick out a project or two, if we could find one or more, that was less deserving than the Keokuk, and strike it from the bill. Our best target, we decided, was something called the General Harrison Lock and Dam on a river feeding into the Tennessee River. I advised the Tennessee congressman, Percy Priest, who was also the Democratic whip of the House of Representatives, of my intent and of the case I had to make. He asked me not to do it, assuring me that he would talk to Senator McKellar of Tennessee, then the chairman of the Senate Appropriations Committee, and that Keokuk would be taken care of. I was disarmed. After the conference between the House and Senate Appropriations Committees was held and some eighteen million dollars for Keokuk granted, I asked an Iowa senator who had been there how it had happened. He reported that it was very strange. Senator McKellar, he said, who seemed to be asleep, had suddenly straightened up and said, "and eighteen million dollars for the Keokuk Lock and Dam," and so ended my career as a budget cutter.

The fifth great "appropriator" was Dan Flood of Pennsylvania. Congressman Flood served on several of the appropriation subcommittees, but made his name, or achieved primary recognition, when on the Defense Department subcommittee. Dan Flood's appearance was striking, if not startling. He was tall, over six feet, of good size, and reputed to have been a boxer of some fame—experience which he called upon when confronted by a coal miner early in his political career. The miner, according to the story, after only one blow from Dan found himself on the floor, flat on his back. Dan also had been an actor, Shakespearean it was said, and he carried that style over into his political oratory. He wore his black hair slicked down in the style of the twenties, and sported an impressive black moustache that was waxed to a fine point. Until his marriage relatively late in life, he wore, as a rule, black or blue suits with pinstripes. After his marriage he blossomed in suits of white, green, yellow, and off colors. His head covering was a black Homburg, and his outer covering in winter was a great black cape. Thus, clothed in black, he had the appearance of a composite ringmaster, a magician, the villain of the old comic strip "Hairbreadth Harry," and an orchestra conductor. It was in this last role that he presented the defense budget for congressional action.

In the two decades following the end of World War II, the defense budget was, compared to the current one, modest—in the range of $50 to $70 billion a year. It was also in these years that the military-industrial complex, the existence of which was noted with a warning by President Eisenhower in his farewell address in 1960, was struggling to institutionalize itself. It was also in these years that the carry-forward costs of World War II had to be faced, as well as the costs of the Korean War, the costs of the early stages of the war in Vietnam, and the burgeoning costs of nuclear arms.

Dan Flood would not have scored high for congressional conduct by recent standards of reform organizations, Congress watchers, and moralizers. He was credited or blamed for having successfully influenced whomever was responsible to run an interstate highway on the Wilkes-Barre side of the Susquehanna, for forcing the military to agree to burn anthracite coal (produced in the mines adjacent to Wilkes-Barre) to heat the barracks of the U.S. troops in Europe under NATO, and for somehow persuading the army or the navy or the air force or the marine corps to send musical units to participate in the periodic "Dan Flood Testimonial Day" parades back in his home district. But to his high credit, he knew the defense budget and was trusted by the leadership of the House of Representatives and by the membership to stand against the power and persuasiveness of the Pentagon. Without this trust, even with the smaller and somewhat simpler appropriations of the fifties and sixties, the members might well have been left in the confusion members of Congress acknowledge today.

Chairmen of various legislative committees also fit into the pattern of leadership and responsibility. There was the hardness but evenhandedness of Carl Vinson, known as "Uncle Carl," the chairman of the Armed Services Committee—the masterful handling of agricultural legislation and the building of a sound farm support program under Chairman Harold Cooley, sometimes referred to as the "sugar and tobacco" chairman. There was Congressman Wright Patman, chairman of the Banking and Currency Committee, the unrelenting enemy of high interest rates and of the chairman of the Federal Reserve Bank, whoever that might be and whatever he might do. And others, including Manny Cellar, chairman of the Judiciary, and especially the chairman of the Ways and Means Committee throughout most of two critical decades, Representative Wilbur Mills of Arkansas.

During four of my ten years in the House of Representatives, I was on this committee (Ways and Means) which, in the House of Representatives, is responsible for revenue raising, for Social Security and related welfare programs, and for tariff policies. The Democratic members of the committee also served as a steering committee for the party, with responsibility for the appointment of the members of other committees.

During the years that Rayburn was Speaker, it was a rule that any tax bill passed by Congress should bear the unmistakable mark of the House of Representatives, as he believed the Constitution intended, and within that context the mark of the Ways and Means Committee. Only minor concessions were to be made on Senate amendments. This position was respected by the senators in tax conferences.

A second rule under Rayburn was that no games should be played with the Ways and Means Committee or with the House of Representatives on tax bills or tax measures. Tentative proposals on other matters might be made by a president and then changed or withdrawn, but on the matter of taxes, no tax program of major significance was to be offered by any president, Republican or Democrat, unless the president was serious about what he proposed and was prepared to defend and support it when it was taken up by the House of Representatives.

Not long after Rayburn was gone, this rule was broken by his former protégé, Lyndon Johnson, who early in his administration sent a tax bill to the House of Representatives as a kind of dove sent out from the ark to see whether spring had come. Finding little response, the President then held the bill in abeyance, an opening step in the irresponsible financing of the Vietnam War.

The rule was again broken when President Carter, who had little knowledge of congressional traditions, sent the Congress a controversial tax bill. The bill included a novel rebate proposal, the essence of which was that taxes would be collected first more or less from everybody, and refunds or, better, rebates would be made later. That is to say, the automobile industry's questionable marketing idea was considered as transferable to government. One member of the Senate who reluctantly had come to support the measure (following much persuasion from the White House) made a speech in favor one day, only to have the President announce the next morning that he no longer supported his own program.

In 1984, the Reagan secretary of the treasury announced proposals for taxation to be acted upon in 1985. The President and his spokespersons followed the presentation by saying that the President had not yet decided whether or not he was for the secretary's tax proposals. By 1986, the tax bill was still adrift.

In the same spirit of disregard for Constitution and tradition, the Reagan Tax Program of his first administration was passed in the Senate before it was enacted in the House, something that would not have been tolerated twenty years earlier in the Rayburn years.

The committee then was run not as a monarchy, but more as a feudal society, in the manner carried over from the Roosevelt New Deal days and continued through the chairmanships of Congressman Robert "Muley" Doughton of North Carolina, of Jere Cooper of Tennessee, who succeeded him, and then of Wilbur Mills.

As in a great hall, facing the witnesses were the chairman and three or four ranking members of each party. As the committee table made a right angle turn, newer members of the committee were left with at best a profile view of the witnesses, but more commonly a view of the back of the witnesses' heads.

The full face members on the Democratic side, the higher nobles in the years of my service on the committee, included Chairman Wilbur Mills, Congressman Hale Boggs of Louisiana, and Congressman Eugene Keogh, later of Keogh Plan fame. Keogh was noted for the Keogh principle, according to which, it was said, he searched the Internal Revenue Code until he found an inequity, and then instead of eliminating the inequity if it gave tax advantages to a limited group, he proposed to spread the "inequity" to all taxpayers. "Universal inequity," he might have said, "is justice." The closest thing to protest in the committee was a move by one of the lower members around the turn to have the witnesses' table moved back a few feet, so that more members might see the witness in profile, and possibly better hear the testimony. The great satisfaction of serving on this committee was the certainty that essentially what the committee did would be approved by the House of Representatives, sustained by the Senate, and, allowing for some Court judgments and Internal Revenue Service interpretations, become law.

The third strong institutional force, or committee, in the House of Representatives in the Rayburn years was the Rules Committee of the House. This was the committee charged with the responsibility of determining what proposals should be brought before the House for consideration, and for determining the conditions under which they should be debated and voted on. The chairman of the committee in the early years of my service in the House of Representatives was Adolph Sabath, a Chicago Democrat.

Adolph was Jewish, short and round of body and head.

His hair, bountiful and white, matched his moustache, clipped and bristling. He looked like how I imagine a proper Jewish Viennese banker should look. His suits were black. He always wore a white shirt and a vest displaying a heavy gold watch chain. He seemed always to be smiling and jovial, but as chairman of the Rules Committee, he was a rock of strength for the Speaker and for the Democratic party. He was a feared poker player, and seemed to carry the skills of that game to his committee work. He was subject to heart attacks, some of which were suspect. I never heard that he had fainted under cover of a heart attack when he held a bad poker hand, but it was noted that the heart attacks he experienced while presiding over the Rules Committee usually occurred when as chairman he was lacking the votes to have his will, and that he usually recovered and reconvened his committee when he had the votes. His rival for power as the ranking Democrat on the committee was Congressman Eugene Cox of Georgia. Cox was long frustrated by Sabath's methods and longevity, frustration and antagonism that led on one occasion to what was called a fist fight between the two on the floor of the House of Representatives. Ironically, Adolph, when he died, did so while Congress was adjourned. Gene Cox succeeded him as chairman, but he in turn died before Congress reconvened. The chairmanship went to Howard Smith of Virginia, known to the Congress as "Judge Smith." The Judge went about his work always as though there were an undesirable and troubling odor in the room.

These were Rayburn's troops, including—after 1948—the delegation of the four of us from Minnesota. Elected by the Democratic Farmer Labor party, we caucused with the

Democrats in Washington and received our committee assignments from that party. Minnesota also elected five Republicans.

The Republican delegation included August Andresen, the original money saver. August would have made Senator Proxmire look like a spendthrift, and could hold a candle to Harry Byrd in his own day. H. Carl Andersen represented a rural area but was the principal spokesman for Main Street —for small town bankers, storekeepers, veterinarians, bottle gas dealers, and water softener salesmen. Harold Hagen represented the far northwestern district of the state, bordering Canada on the one side and North Dakota on the other. He was a former Farmer laborite, and when the merger of that party with the Democratic party took place, he opted for the Republican party and survived for many years—although his record reflected more the spirit of his district than it did the reality of the Republicans. There was much in his heavy Scandinavian approach of flat lands, of a flooding Red River of the North, of dust storms that blew over from North Dakota across the Red River, and of blizzards that roared down from Canada. A side interest of Harold's, something denied him in Minnesota, was an occasional bet on the horses running on the Maryland tracks.

The fourth member of the Republican delegation was Walter Judd, the great defender of Chiang Kai-shek. Walter had been a medical missionary in China and was not loath to tell of how dedicated Communists were, to the extent that they had tried to convert him, Walter Judd, as he stood over them, scalpel in hand.

The fifth Republican was Joe O'Hara, a staunch conservative; Joe was what the Irish call a "good hater." His special target was liberal Republicans, especially the head of the liberal internationalists Harold Stassen and anyone who had anything to do with Harold. The contingent were formidable, not as a group, but individually.

Farmer Labor Democrats, in our year of great success, 1948, elected four out of the nine House members, and to the Senate that year Hubert Humphrey. We were so full of good spirit that at the victory banquet following the election, the speeches ran nigh onto midnight, with the recurring refrain of "four out of nine," to the point at which a woman leaving the hotel, when quiet finally dropped on the multitudes, was heard to say, "Thank God we didn't elect all nine of them, or we'd have been kept here until dawn." And well they might have been.

The "four out of nine," were led by Congressman John Blatnik, who was senior to all others in the delegation, having been elected to Congress in 1946. John represented the northern part of the state, the area known as the "iron range," where for years the principal industry has been the mining, processing, and shipping of iron ore. John's father was a Yugoslav who had come to Minnesota as an immigrant to work in the mines. John, like many other miners' sons and daughters—Yugoslavs (both Croatians and Serbs), Italians, Poles, some Finns—in politics, had moved up farther and faster than most children of immigrants to the United States.

The second member of our delegation was Roy Weir, a labor leader who had headed the stage hands union. Roy was an uncompromising union man with no respect for management, nor for captains of industry or finance, and little respect for the language except to use it well, if not correctly. One of the best words in his vocabulary, and an often used word of his own making, was "co-allusion." It was the word he used to denote the Republican-Dixiecrat combination. Customarily, it was used with an adjective or two—a "damned co-allusion" if Roy was only modestly aroused, stronger adjectives if truly disturbed.

The third member of our delegation was Fred Marshall, who represented the agricultural heart of the state. Fred was a farmer and looked the part. His cheeks were always, it seemed, wind burned, as though he had been plowing in a raw March, and his eyes clear blue, sizing up crops, cattle, and people. He knew where people had come from. A national election expert approached Fred asking why Lemke had done so well as a presidential candidate on the Social Justice ticket in an area of Fred's district. The expert, looking —it seemed—for some socialist trend or base, was informed by Fred that it might well be because it was the area in which Lemke had been born.

Fred's approach to political problems was equally direct, elemental, and clear. When he retired he set up a small sawmill on his farm, on the banks of the Crow River, as there was a good stand of native oak in need of harvesting. Fred thought that, as a rule, one should harvest what grew on one's land.

These were good men with whom to go to Congress, or as Lyndon Johnson was accustomed to saying, "to go to the well with," a frontier reference to the task of going outside the stockade to fetch water. I went as the fourth member of that 1949 delegation.

My first political test of that Congress, the Eighty-first, was on the sensitive and complicated issue of government security. Senator Joseph McCarthy had not come into full strength yet, but the anti-Communism, pro-security issue was running strongly, especially in the House of Representatives and its instrument, the House Committee on Un-American Activities. Noteworthy committee members included Republican Parnell Thomas of New Jersey and Martin Dies of Texas.

The security bill was in fact offered by the Truman administration, which also gave it legislative sanction. The original bill proposed that in sensitive agencies, the ordinary rules of the civil service need not be applied. The administration indicated what departments and agencies it thought sensitive. Before Congress had finished with the bill, almost every government department and agency had been included. At the time I was a member of the Post Office and Civil Service Committee, which had jurisdiction over the legislation and had held hearings and reported to the Congress a limited and responsible piece of legislation. As the Communist baiters endeavored to broaden the scope of the bill, I, out of some regard for my committee's work but mainly out of a deeper belief, offered an amendment. My deeper belief was fresh as I was from academic life where I had often spoken of the near sacredness of the person and of the need for society to distinguish among persons, in keeping with the ideas of Emanuel Mounier's book, *The Personalist Manifesto.* And I remembered Charles Peguy's observation on the Dreyfus case, that if an injustice against one person was allowed to stand unchallenged in a society, that the whole of that society would be corrupted. My amendment was, I thought, clear and modest, providing that any person who was dismissed (according to the very liberal standards for dismissal) from jobs in the sensitive agencies should have preference for reemployment in other nonsensitive agencies and government offices. The amendment was not accepted, and so seemed to fall among the lost legislative efforts. There it remained, unnoticed through my 1950 campaign for reelection. By 1952, it had been discovered and made the central point of a campaign to defeat me. My opponent, a neophyte in politics, had responded it seems to an advertisement by the Republicans seeking a candidate. He yielded himself to his handlers, and in the years since has habitually apologized for the campaign. The St. Paul paper had always opposed me, but never with the virulence of the 1952 campaign, intensified possibly because my opponent was a nephew of the owner-publisher. In any case, the campaign was marked by full-page advertisements, some signed by the outstanding lawyers in St. Paul, charging, in effect, that my amendment was treasonous. There were flyers carrying the challenging question "Is Your Congressman a Traitor?" And a television commercial appeared, among the earliest political uses of that medium, showing my opponent interviewing two soldiers home on leave from Korea. "And how did you feel when you came home and found that your congressman was giving aid and comfort to the enemy?" he asked. The soldiers expressed their distress, of course.

In a major debate scheduled at the Hamline Methodist Church, located on the campus of Hamline University, Minnesota's Methodist university, my opponent did not appear but sent a substitute—a leading Republican lawyer and party official named Warren Burger. The compelling line in Burger's presentation was that the kind of people I had tried to protect, even minimally, had to be hacked out of government with a "pick-axe, not with a scalpel." Some seventeen years later, in 1969, when he was nominated to be chief justice of the United States Supreme Court, I voted against his nomination. Only two other senators voted with me, Stephen Young of Ohio and Gaylord Nelson of Wisconsin.

I learned a great deal in that campaign about surrendering to pressure and, also, about courage in politics. The surrender came principally from persons dependent, economically, on the establishment: corporate employees, established lawyers, college presidents. One could see the Niemueller principle working: each group and each person protecting its own interests, taking the easy way. But there was opposition, bold and courageous, involving risk of position, of economic security, even of family relationships. The head of the religion department of Macalester College, a Presbyterian college in St. Paul, Robert McAfee Brown, incensed by the attacks, offered himself as a campaign worker. "I will do anything," he said, "write letters, make speeches, work in the mailing room . . ."

Wives whose husbands had signed the advertisements against me called to apologize, and some offered to work on the campaign. At least one sent her husband to the campaign headquarters to apologize and to offer to write a letter disclaiming the advertisement. Even a number of the employees of the paper rose up against their publisher, raising money to print a counter paper, writing copy for it, and even printing a mock issue. I discouraged them from publishing it, partly because I was quite certain that we would win without it, partly because of its content, and partly because of my concern for the risks to those who were willing to go on record, although this last concern was minimal. One should not discourage rational heroism or courage.

Most courageous of all was a statement sent to me by the top minority employee of the Post Office and Civil Service Committee of the House of Representatives, George Murray, stating clearly that the case against me was fraudulent. Speaking as a Republican staff member, he ran the risk of dismissal, and even of blackballing. He was not, and has gone on to a long and productive career in government service. With the passage of years, and especially in the antiwar campaign of 1968 when other administration officials—not Republicans—could have come forward as George did to clarify the record and set it straight, but did not, the action of George Murray, in my book of records, remains a clear act of political courage.

The experience in 1952, I think, encouraged and heartened me in my subsequent challenges to established pressures, especially to charges of being weak or stupid in assessing the threat of Communism. I knew that one could stand against these forces and that one need not and should not believe that there were none who would stand with him.

Although in my mind the amendment dealing with reemployment of civil servants in nonsensitive positions had little to do with the Communist threat and seemed to me a simple act of justice involving no threat to the national interest, it also reflected my opinion of the time that the domestic Communist threat was greatly exaggerated. In politics at the time, being a Catholic was helpful since it was assumed that a Catholic was anti-Communist and also that Catholics understood the threat. My limited exposure to Communists (I missed the Spanish Civil War and the Lin-

coln Brigade liberal involvement by a few years) on the
university campus in graduate school had not moved me to
fear and trembling. My rough judgment was that most students, the normal, average and the clearly intelligent ones,
were not much moved by Communist ideology. Its support
and advocacy came rather from those on the edge of higher
intelligence, who were looking for the security of a closed,
simple system.

Exposure to the two kinds of Communists who were involved in Minnesota politics in the post–World War II period could only impress one with their incompetence and
with the internal, mostly personal conflicts between them.
Minnesota seemed undisturbed by their existence. In the
forties and fifties, the Minnesota State Fair Board allowed
both the Socialist Workers and the Socialist Labor party to
operate booths at the fair. One booth showed a thermome-
terlike measure of the rise of the red influence; the other, a
globe, which my then-young daughter took for a Sherman-
Williams paint advertisement, with the Communist countries colored red.

When one of the lists of suspected subversives was published, a member of the faculty of St. Catherine's College in
St. Paul, in noting one name, observed, "I was in graduate
school with him, and if he is part of the threat, we have little
to worry about."

Communism was not overlooked in the curriculum at St.
John's when I was there as a student and as a teacher. It was
taught, not as a significant philosophical or ideological
movement, but as a historical movement, subject to historical judgment. Marx's writings were read along with Aris-
totle, St. Thomas, Maritain, Nietzsche, and other political
philosophers.

That background—Minnesota and education, plus the fact that Catholics were assumed to understand the threat of Communism—may have given me more courage in what came to be called the McCarthy period. I did not look on what I did as requiring courage, but as a reasonably proper, moral response.

My first sight of Richard Nixon was in 1949, when he was still a member of the House of Representatives in his second term, but running for the Senate to which he was elected in 1950. His campaign was against Helen Douglas, and anti-Communism weighed strongly as an issue. Nixon, whom I did not know, and of whom I knew little, seemed euphoric as he entered the chamber one day. He began to make a kind of triumphal round among Republican members, smiling and shaking hands enthusiastically. Some Democrats crossed the aisle to greet him. He seemed ecstatic and was, as I discovered. He was carrying the word of the conviction of Alger Hiss, a credit which he took himself.

My first more or less formal challenge to the Communist baiters—actually, they were not so much Communist baiters as baiters of persons who believed in freedom of speech, assembly, privacy, and in the constitutional principle that persons were innocent until proven guilty—was in a speech in the early spring of 1950, within a month or two of Senator Joe McCarthy's famous Wheeling, West Virginia, speech of February 1950. The speech Joe gave was actually a rewrite of a speech made by Nixon earlier and given to Senator McCarthy as a basic text. In February 1977, twenty-seven years later, Al Friendly of the *Washington Post* attempted to explain and excuse the press for its building up of the whole anti-Communist cold war attitude in the early fifties. Friendly, in his article, acknowledged that within a month after the Wheeling speech, it was clear that the Senator was using fraudulent material. Yet major newspapers continued to give the charges front page attention.

"At the outset," Friendly said, "for the first week or so and before they could be examined, McCarthy's charges appeared to be of the most profound national significance and might, quite possibly, be true." The Senate panicked and held hearings. For the press to have ignored the most newsworthy event in Congress (however phony the thing was beginning to look), the focus of congressional and, almost at once, national attention, was preposterous. Friendly was right. No one expected the press to ignore the story. The point of criticism then, and in retrospect, was the exploitation and overpublication of nearly every charge that was made.

In contrast, some twenty years later when Congressman Hale Boggs charged that the FBI was spying on members of Congress (this long before the ABSCAM project was set up to entrap members of Congress), the press called upon the congressman to name the people involved and to publicly prove his point. He did not, or possibly could not. One can only speculate as to what might have happened if the press had insisted on comparable proof from Senator McCarthy in 1950.

My post-Wheeling speech was made to the Holy Name Societies of Montgomery County, Maryland, bordering Washington, D.C., and making up one of its major suburbs. The meeting was outdoors on a school ground. I was in my first term in Congress, of no special fame, and therefore I was surprised to note how well covered my speech evidently was going to be. This was before television had become the

instrument of political coverage, but press and radio reporters were there in numbers with recording equipment. I sur-
mised that whoever promoted the Holy Name Society,
which is dedicated to protecting and defending the Holy
Name from abuse, had impressive press connections until, as
I went on with my speech—a pertinent one, I thought, to the
issue of name calling, in which my basic thesis was that God
could pretty well take care of his own name, and that the
Holy Name Society should concern itself at least in some
measure with the names of lesser beings, even of politicians
and employees of the State Department—I noted that the
equipment that had been set up was now being withdrawn,
trucks loaded, and reporters fading away from the school
yard. They quickly had realized that they were covering the
wrong McCarthy, and even though my speech was a challenge, although somewhat indirect, to what Joseph
McCarthy was saying, the press had no interest in it. Contrary to what Al Friendly wrote in 1977, in 1950 the press
was looking for McCarthy headlines.

In November of 1952, I debated Senator Joseph McCarthy
on the NBC television program "American Forum of the
Air." The moderator, Theodore Granick, told me that he had
asked me to debate because no one in the Senate would
accept the invitation. I hoped to include a few excerpts from
the transcript, but have been unable to find one, either in my
own files or from the archives of NBC, the Library of Congress or the Museum of Broadcasting. Evidently, the television and media powers of the time did not consider the
debate significant. It was not covered by the political reporters in Washington, but by the local television reviewer, who
gave me credit for holding the senator at bay. Although I had

been warned against going on the program by some friends, and begged not to do so by others, the effects were minimal, if at all measurable. Before the debate began, Senator McCarthy approached me and said, "We don't want this to become an Irish brawl." It didn't.

It was a curious time. Vito Marcantonio, a congressman from New York, was a radical liberal. Conservatives in campaigns would publish records of what percentage of a congressman's votes were the same as those of Marcantonio, suggesting that this was a record of un-Americanism, if not pro-Communism. Most of Marcantonio's votes were the same as those of liberal Democrats. A newspaper notice that his wallet had been stolen or lost reported that he especially wanted to recover two religious medals, one of Mother Cabrini, an Italian-born American who had recently been canonized by the Catholic Church, and the second a medal that he had received when he was confirmed in the Church. Only four or five members of the House of Representatives rose to eulogize him and comment on his person and record after his death in 1954.

The Communist hunt knew few if any limits. In the summer of 1956, I was asked by an old friend, John Cogley, if I would accompany him and introduce him to the House Committee on Un-American Activities, which had issued a subpoena, requiring his attendance. At the time, Cogley was on the executive staff of the Fund for the Republic, whose president then was Robert Hutchins. Cogley had been executive editor of *Commonweal,* a magazine published by lay Catholics, when he was approached by Hutchins to do a study of blacklisting in the entertainment industry. The report was published in two volumes, *Blacklisting: Movies* and *Blacklisting: Radio-Television.*

Most of the code words currently in use by the Communist hunters were used to attack Cogley, who was in no way a Communist, and to attack the report, which was prepared under strict academic standards. The report was called "bogus," the blacklisting referred to as "alleged blacklisting." *Commonweal* magazine was identified as left of center, the Fund for the Republic as "ultraleftist" (ultra was a big word), and Hutchins as leftist. One of Cogley's associates was called a "one-time" member of the Young Communist League.

The Cogley investigation was evidence that the House Un-American Activities Committee was running out of subjects for investigation and had lost its public position as the major anti-Communist force in Congress, to the Senate, and especially to Senator Joseph McCarthy.

During the years immediately following the election of President Truman in 1948, substantial progress was made in advancing the programs advocated in the campaign of that year. Following the election of President Eisenhower and the increased Republican strength in the Congress, there was a slowdown of legislative progress. It was a period of drift within the Democratic party, as there was—especially after the second defeat of Adlai Stevenson in 1956—no strong voice to state policy and no person to provide leadership. Paul Butler, the national chairman of the Democratic party, tried hard to establish a position for the party and to give a liberal direction to party policy. His efforts were not successful, and gradually the focus of the power within the party heads shifted to the Congress, eventually to the Senate majority leader, Lyndon Johnson.

The "go along, get along" philosophy seemed to be taking over the Democratic party. Therefore, in 1957, Congressman

Lee Metcalf of Montana and I concluded that it had become necessary for the liberal Democrats in the House to assert themselves, at least as far as stating their position on the important issues, reaffirming the platform of 1948, and doing something about it. Other House members joined with us, particularly Congressman Frank Thompson of New Jersey and Congressman John Blatnick of Minnesota. We drafted what we called "A Liberal Manifesto," covering six vital areas of political action: education, civil rights, health, housing, foreign aid, and atomic policy. Eventually, eighty members of Congress subscribed to the declaration. Our purpose and commitment was to do what we could to have each of these issues at least presented for some action by the House of Representatives. Although our group was labeled "Marauders" or "Mavericks" by the press, we did not look upon ourselves as disruptive of the party, but rather as its principal supporters. Eventually, the group developed into a formal and structured organization within the Congress, called the Democratic Study Group, and went on to become the central planning and directing force of the Democratic party in the House of Representatives.

This was the closest thing to a revolt against Rayburn's leadership. The Manifesto became a guide and challenge to the Democrats in Congress. For the next twenty years the House of Representatives was a good institution. Seniority was respected. Committee chairmen had power, or the appearance of it. Offices were not overstaffed. Subcommittees were discouraged, as were special committees.

There were several lines of defense between a member and unreasonable demands of his or her constituency. He or she might blame a committee of Congress for delay and

obstruction, or blame a chairman, and beyond that blame
seniority. If an authorization for something requiring money
had been achieved, the problem of getting the money appro-
priated remained, and the appropriations committees could
be blamed. Or responsibility might be placed on the Rules
Committee.

The House was not a home exactly, but it was an effective
enough political and governmental body.

PART II

SENATORIAL POLITICS

THE IMMEDIATE post–World War II Senate was the Senate of coalition politics, a condition reinforced by the Eisenhower "hold the line" administration. Most of the strong senators were conservative—Harry Byrd, Tom Connally of Texas, Richard Russell of Georgia and his senior, Senator Walter George, Carter Glass of Virginia, and Pat McCarran from Nevada. Among the Republicans there were Arthur Vandenberg of Michigan, Eugene Millikin of Colorado, Ralph Flanders of Vermont, Styles Bridges of New Hampshire, Robert Taft of Ohio, Irving Ives of New York, and Henry Cabot Lodge of Massachusetts.

The Senate was the last primitive society in the Western world. Its controlling principle was seniority, a principle not always applied but always in reserve if difficult circumstances were to arise. Possessing an office, title, even space established a first right which was very difficult to deny or circumvent. Committee memberships and office space were chosen or assigned according to a complicated code of prior rights or experience. Even the assignment of committee memberships and office space to incoming members was based on formalized and traditionally accepted rules. Former senators returning to the Senate ranked above those with no such experience. Former House of Representatives members were given precedence over other newcomers. Former governors and state legislature members were given minor credits against persons with no political experience, and so the rules of distinction ran on, down to alphabetical distinctions.

In the Senate, trial by ordeal in the form of the filibuster was the ultimate test. It was essentially a defensive weapon, supported principally by Southern Democrats, a carryover from the Civil War and post–Civil War politics. Filibustering was also supported, more or less by tradition, by senators from very small states on the grounds that it was a kind of equalizer, offsetting the power of the larger states, which have more members in the House of Representatives.

Civility, too, was the rule of the time. A member who, in speaking, disparaged another member—particularly if he questioned the member's integrity and high character— might be denied the right to continue speaking, the ultimate deprivation for a senator. Questioning another member's intelligence or accuracy of knowledge might get past censorship, but not any questioning of purity of motives. The margin of difference was demonstrated in the statement of one member of Congress that he had "minimal high regard" for his opponent. Anything less than that would have been censurable.

The idea of the Senate as a continuing body also had its roots in primitive society, a kind of modern version of sacred fires and vestal virgins. The Senate application of this idea was made in arguing against allowing rule changes by majority votes at the beginning of a new Congress, something allowed the House. The argument made against this practice in the Senate was that only one-third of the Senate was elected in each bi-annual election; two-thirds carried over from previous elections. The filibuster rule, therefore, applied to rule changes as it did to legislative matters. The argument of some opponents of the filibuster rule was not accepted as overriding the ancient rule. That rule seemed to be based on the accepted belief that as long as senators were free to speak without limitation, the Republic would survive. When it was pointed out to Senator Russell in one of the early civil rights debates that the Constitution of the Confederacy provided for a limitation on debate, he responded that that limitation might have been responsible for the Confederacy's having lost the Civil War.

The keepers of the flame, the guardians of Senate tradition, were principally the Southern senators. Their reasons were basically two: one, it gave the South a line of defense against the passage of civil rights legislation; and two, with the presidency denied to Southern politicians, the Senate was the end of political achievement (the ultimate goal) of Southern politicians, and the protection and preservation of the traditional Senate was essential to ensure the fullest political participation by its members.

The internal operation of the Senate in those years was more primitive than it was classical. The Platonic concept of the guardians was that they should be individually pure and unattached. Plato held that there should be no particular groupings, no cliques, no inner circle among them, no establishment within the establishment. A few senators held this classical view, most notably Senator Morse of Oregon who, within the course of his service in the Senate, was a Republican, an Independent, and a Democrat.

The more common disposition was to become members of "the club," an inner corps which operated—depending on one's point of view—above or below simple party identification. There were satellite rings in orbit around the club: a Republican one, a liberal Democrat one, and a third, referred to in the fifties by some as "The White Citizens' Council," made up of Southern Democrats.

Whereas the Senate does, and did, have a comprehensive set of procedural rules, most of its business was conducted under unanimous consent. Regular recourse to the rules by any senator was looked upon as weakness on his part, much as "unsportsmanlike conduct" is looked upon in athletics. A cloakroom rule was that a senator's case could be judged without looking at the content, simply by noting how often and with what intensity he quoted from the Bible (a sign of some weakness), how often he went to the Constitution for help (also a sign of weakness), and finally his recourse to the Senate rules (the ultimate sign of weakness).

Senator Lyndon Johnson

The election of Lyndon Johnson as majority leader of the Senate in 1954 was an indication of structural and functional changes to come. Johnson was essentially a pragmatist regarding operations, a practicing barbarian relative to institutions. His talents and activist drive probably would have suited him better as a majority leader or Speaker of the House, or as a prime minister in a parliamentary government with party discipline and a cabinet made up of people with some independent political power, than as President under the Constitution of the United States.

Johnson as majority leader of the Senate did not favor many formal changes in the rules. He saw enough latitude and freedom within the rules to do what he wished. He was a staunch defender of the filibuster, possibly out of the commitment he had made to Southern senators when he was chosen as majority leader, and possibly out of personal commitment—or as a position continuing that which he had held as a senator from Texas. He also believed that a determined majority could break a filibuster if it set its mind and will to the work. He was right. Most of the basic civil rights legislation was passed while the filibuster rule was still in effect, and also while major committees were controlled by the Southern chairmen in the Senate—including the Judiciary Committee, with James Eastland of Mississippi as its chairman. The filibuster rule was not changed until 1975.

Johnson's attitude toward the filibuster and how to deal with it was shown in a conversation with him early in 1963, while he was still vice president. During his vice presidency, Lyndon kept a large office just off the Senate floor, the same office he had occupied as majority leader. Senator Mansfield, who succeeded Johnson as majority leader, did not claim the office space of his predecessor, but took over more modest quarters somewhat further removed from the entrance to the Senate chamber.

It was not uncommon for the vice president to emerge from his office just as the Senate was adjourning in the late afternoon or early evening, and, standing in the door of his office, call a passing senator or two—or even more—into his chambers. On one such afternoon, he waved five of us into his room; Senator Humphrey, Senator Muskie, two Michigan senators, and me. It was mid-January 1963, the Senate having convened following the elections of 1962. The vice president, after reviewing some of his accomplishments as majority leader in passing civil rights legislation, moved on to the matter of civil rights legislation of 1963. He was in favor of action, and indicated that the Kennedy administration had decided to put off a serious civil rights legislation battle, possibly until after the 1964 presidential election. Johnson was ready with a medical report on all senators likely to support a filibuster on civil rights. Senator Byrd of Virginia, he pointed out, had just gotten out of the hospital. Senator Ellender of Louisiana was in the hospital. Senator Russell of Georgia, the established floor leader of the anti–civil rights bloc, was ill with what he (Russell) thought to be cancer of the throat. Johnson went on in this manner, concluding by saying that only two of the senators who would fight vigorously in a filibuster were able bodied, and expressed his belief that a filibuster could be broken in two weeks. With the filibuster rule in effect and with a thin liberal pro–civil rights majority in the Senate, Johnson had succeeded in passing the Civil Rights Act of 1957, an achievement which he is reported to have looked upon as his greatest achievement as majority leader of the Senate. Truly it was a masterful piece of legislative work, for the pro–civil rights strength in the Senate was marginal, and the Eisenhower administration but moderately committed to the passage of civil rights legislation. The Civil Rights Act of 1957 set up the Civil Rights Commission, established the Civil Rights Division in the Department of Justice, and dealt more broadly with voting rights. The filibuster associated with it lasted thirty-eight days, broken into two segments.

Signs of change in the Senate were evident in the elections of the early fifties. But it was the election of 1958 that brought to the Senate strength of numbers sufficient to change the Senate and set the stage for the passage of additional civil rights legislation, changing the concept of the federal judiciary from a regional court system to a national one. Senator William Proxmire was elected from Wisconsin, replacing Joseph McCarthy, who had died. Frank Church from Idaho, John Carroll from Colorado (both elected in 1956), and Ralph Yarborough from Texas added strength.

There was no great organized effort before 1958 on the part of the Democratic party to increase its strength in the Senate. The candidates ran more or less independently of each other, and those elected included a former governor, a lieutenant governor, a mayor, a district attorney, and an unusually high number of House members, some with seniority (seven in all). The former House members may have been moved to run for the Senate out of boredom with the House, as was reflected in a remark made by John Kennedy as he sat—a member of the House—listening to a speech (or possibly waiting for it to end) before a vote: "I suppose that if one doesn't want to work, this is as good a job as any to have." If not boredom, possibly the former House members ran for the Senate because they were tired of having to go through a campaign every two years—even in safe districts the campaign is a trial for the candidate. But in 1958 most of the House candidates for Senate were moved to run, as

I was, with the primary purpose of doing something positive about civil rights legislation, which, with the exception of the 1957 legislation, had languished in the Senate while tension and danger of violence mounted in the country.

Although civil rights was the most important matter facing the country, it was not the dominant or controlling issue in many of the Senate races; in the Midwest and West agriculture was clearly seen as more important. In those states the Eisenhower secretary of agriculture, Ezra Taft Benson, became the incarnation of agricultural problems. Benson and the agricultural issue may have influenced the outcome of the election more than civil rights, but the consequence of the election for the advancement of civil rights legislation was more significant than its bearing on farm policy.

The fact that about half of the newly elected Democratic members of the Senate that assembled in January of 1958 were former members of the House affected committee assignments and the tone of the Democratic majority. It also affected the Democratic leader, Lyndon Johnson, who, in making committee assignments, was somewhat limited by what the House members had been and what committees they had served on before coming to the Senate. Dealing with someone like Claire Engel, who had been chairman of the Interior Committee of the House, was something quite different from what it would have been had Claire been a newly elected Senate member without House background asking to be put on the Interior Committee of the Senate. Many new members came with claims established by their records and achievements. They could ask for what they deserved, rather than for benevolent treatment by the majority leader.

Having served for four years on the House Ways and Means Committee by the time I was elected to the Senate in 1958, I asked for assignment to the comparable committee in the Senate—the Finance Committee. I was given the post, but not without the word getting to me through some Texans that Lyndon had something to do with my being assigned. Undoubtedly he did, but his action was consistent with his general policy of rewarding rather than punishing, or pleasing rather than offending. Not assigning me to the committee I had asked for, or not assigning other former House members to their requested committees, would have been difficult for the leader to explain or defend. Ten years later, in the early stages of my challenge to President Johnson on the Vietnam War, the word came to me that Lyndon considered me ungrateful in view of the fact that ten years earlier he had given me the Finance Committee post (even though that committee had nothing to do with the war, directly or indirectly).

Lyndon liked to accumulate points, even small ones. As one member with a background in handling cattle said, "If Lyndon couldn't get a hide-brand (one burned into the skin), he would settle for a hair-brand." A hair-brand lasts only until the singed hair grows back, and thus is neither deep nor permanent. Pursuing this metaphor in another application, the same member of the Senate described the barbecues on the Johnson ranch as not having started out to be barbecues, but as branding parties that had gotten out of control.

The press accepted, properly, that the committee assignments generally had been fairly made, with the exception of those given to Senator Edmund Muskie. By report, the relatively poor committee assignments given to the former governor of Maine resulted from his refusal after intense persuasive efforts on the part of the majority leader, to promise to support the continuation of the filibuster. This may be true if the report of the meeting between the majority leader and the newly elected senator from Maine is reasonably accurate. The Johnson argument, as given, was the traditional one that senators from small states should support the filibuster. When Senator Muskie said he was on record against the filibuster, Johnson countered by saying that in the Senate, one is not committed to a vote until he has heard all the arguments and the roll is called. Lyndon, evidently believing that his arguments had prevailed, said to Muskie as the latter was about to leave the meeting, "By the way, how do you intend to vote on the filibuster?" Muskie is said to have replied, "I don't know, I haven't heard all the arguments and the roll is not being called."

It was after this meeting, or one like it, that Senator Muskie made another pointed observation. Lyndon, in trying to move others to agree with him, used physical persuasion in addition to intellectual and moral appeals. He was hard on other people's coat lapels. If one were shorter than Lyndon he was inclined to move up close and lean over the subject of his persuasive efforts. A classical picture of this method in use was one of Lyndon standing over Senator Green of Rhode Island, a very slight man who served in the Senate in his nineties. Senator Theodore Green was bent over backward so far that he seemed to be defying the laws of gravity. If a senator were taller than the majority leader (few were), he would come at him from below, somewhat like a badger, fighting up. Senator Muskie was taller. He emerged from one meeting with Johnson with the observation that he had not known until this meeting why people had the hair in their nostrils trimmed.

There were strong men in the Senate during Johnson's period as leader, strong in themselves and set on holding on to traditional power. Johnson dissipated their power, in part, by changing the Senate into a kind of House of Representatives. Seniority in making assignments to committees, or in transfers, was not always honored. Special committees and subcommittees became more common, thus weakening the power of regular committee chairmen. Prolonged debates were not encouraged. Lyndon preferred to have things worked out well before they were brought to the floor of the Senate for consideration. Pro forma speeches began to replace serious debate. Roll call votes proliferated, and quantitative measures of achievement were emphasized.

The majority leader periodically would issue reports to the press regarding the number of bills that had been passed, often contrasting the achievement with the record made by other Congresses. His reputation for knowing how a vote was going to go was well earned. As one member of the Senate observed early in the Mansfield leadership period, when a vote had been lost by one or two and Senator Mansfield made the closing speech for the losing effort, "If Lyndon were leader we would not have lost it by one or two votes. If Lyndon was going to lose a vote, he would not have lost it by one or two votes, but by five or six, and would not have made the closing speech unless he was sure he was going to win." He had the gift, if a situation began to get out of hand, of creating premeditated chaos, thereby confusing the opposition and buying time to reorganize his own case.

With Johnson as President and Senator Mansfield as majority leader of the Senate, two crucial pieces of civil rights legislation were passed. The Civil Rights Act of 1964 prohibited discrimination in public accommodations and in programs receiving federal financial assistance; it prohibited discrimination by employers and by unions, set up an Equal Employment Opportunity Commission, and strengthened the laws for enforcing voting rights and school and public facilities desegregation. The Senate filibuster lasted for fifty-seven days, possibly the greatest and most significant filibuster in the history of the Senate as well as the longest. The 1965 Civil Rights law authorized the attorney general to appoint federal examiners to register voters under prescribed conditions and increased the penalties for interference with voter rights. It was subject to a filibuster of only nine days, evidence that the filibuster as a device for stopping the passage of civil rights legislation was no longer effective.

U.S. SENATORS:

A GOODLY COMPANY

WHEN I BECAME A MEMBER of the Finance Committee in January of 1959, the chairman was Harry Byrd, Sr., of Virginia. At the time I knew Senator Byrd only by reputation as a stern conservative, a watchdog of the treasury, and an unrelenting segregationalist. He was all of these, and at the same time unaggressive, considerate, and above all, as chairman of the committee, utterly fair, the fairest chairman of the ten or twelve under whom I served in both the House and the

Senate. Byrd was for open committee work. When the reformers moved against closed executive committee hearings,
Byrd was scarcely subject to criticism. The rule of his committee was that any action taken in closed session could be
subject to a roll call vote at the request of a single member
of the committee. The results of the vote—the way each
member voted—would be announced to the press and the
public following the end of an executive session. Almost
every controversial action was subjected to a roll call vote,
usually called for by Senator Paul Douglas of Illinois, who
wished to expose conservative voters, or by John Williams
of Delaware, wishing to expose liberal voters—although
both might ask for roll calls on the same matter, especially
if it related to oil depletion allowances. The policy of taking
votes on request of a single member and of making those
votes public was abandoned soon after Senator Byrd was
succeeded as chair of the committee.

In 1961, following the election of John Kennedy as President, there was an incipient move to deny the committee
chairmanship to Harry Byrd because he had supported
Nixon in the campaign. There was little support for the
move on the part of the Democratic members of the committee, and it soon died out. While the ouster was being talked
about, I told Chairman Byrd, half in jest, that if he were
dispossessed I would resign from the committee. I did not
expect to be put to the test, but probably would have resigned if the chairmanship had been taken from him. My
reasons were twofold: first, I had marked well his fairness,
and second, because of my theoretical position that the Senate did not lend itself to strict partisan organization as did
the House—due to its size and, more importantly, because

of its constitutional functions. In any case, Senator Byrd accepted my statement to him as the fullest expression of support he had received from any senator.

Byrd seemed reconciled to the Kennedy presidency, and the President to the senator. At Senator Byrd's annual noon lunch, given on his farm in Virginia in April just at the time that the apple blossoms were in full flower, President Kennedy was invited. The President flew in a helicopter and arrived in a shower of apple blossom petals, much to the pleasure of Senator Byrd, who seemed almost overcome by the President's visit. The visit, however, did little to change Byrd's political views.

My second or supplemental committee during my first term in the Senate was the Public Works Committee, given me because every senator as a rule had to be on two committees. Minnesota, as I noted earlier in writing of my House service, was not very deeply involved in public works of the traditional kind.

Service on the committee was rewarding on two counts, however. We passed the first comprehensive clean water bill, only to have it vetoed by President Eisenhower. It was passed again under John Kennedy and signed into law. Clean water and environmental protection became so popular that it stirred a controversy over which committee of the Congress should have jurisdiction over "solid sewage." The Public Works Committee claimed jurisdiction because most of the sewage processing facilities and other construction relative to handling the product involved public works. The Interior Committee claimed jurisdiction because most of the disposal projects involved the use of waterways, land condemnation, and so forth. It was clear that environmental protection had arrived as a major issue when Senate committees began to compete for jurisdiction over and responsibility for solid sewage.

Service on the committee was rewarding for a second reason, namely, its chairman, Senator Dennis Chavez of New Mexico. Senator Chavez, of Spanish background, loyally supported by his people in New Mexico, had what was probably the safest and surest seat in the Senate. He was there from 1935 until his death in 1962. As a result of his security and because of his courage, he was called upon to undertake what for other senators might be politically dangerous projects.

Some of the things Senator Chavez undertook to do for the Senate were of great national significance, some of political significance, some of importance to internal Senate operations. The most noteworthy of his undertakings, of national significance, was his speech on May 12, 1950, in which he challenged the persons who were exploiting the Communist issue, especially one Louis Budenz, who claimed special authority as a former Communist who had become a convert to Catholicism. In his speech, Chavez said, "For the first time in nineteen years in the Congress, I make the deliberate point of referring to my religion. I speak as a Roman Catholic. Nowadays a man who claims he is a Catholic is accorded special attention and authority when discussing Communism. For this reason," Chavez said, "a special obligation is imposed on anyone speaking on this subject while enjoying the status afforded by the Church."

He then went on to mark Louis Budenz for special attention. Budenz, he said, "has been speaking with special emphasis as a Catholic, investing his appearances and utterances with an added sanctity by virtue of the fact that he recently went through the forms of conversion to Catholicism." Then, at the high point of his speech, Senator Chavez said, "My ancestors brought the cross to this hemisphere. Louis Budenz has been using this cross as a club."

It could not be said that Communist hunters were destroyed by the Chavez speech, but those who had been afraid to challenge them were encouraged. A month later, a group of Republican senators joined under the leadership of Senator Margaret Smith of Maine in issuing their declaration of conscience on the same subject.

The final act of service in the Senate by Senator Chavez came shortly before his death. It was not an act of high statesmanship, or one involving great national issues, but one of rather lowly, some would say, unimportant service to the Senate. At issue was money to build a new swimming pool in the Senate gymnasium. There was a pool in the gym, but it was not much more than a large bathtub, possibly twelve by twelve. I was in it alone one day when Senator Stennis approached and asked whether I minded his getting in with me. "I will stand still," he said.

Economizers in the Senate, led by Senator Proxmire, had been looking to make an issue of cutting out the money for the pool and in the course of the year had not been able to target the appropriation. The Senate had now come down to the closing minutes of a session and was considering a supplemental appropriations bill. The economizers figured that the money they had been watching for must be in the bill and challenged the senator who was managing the bill on the Senate floor, Senator John Stennis. One after another they took the floor demanding to know whether there was any money hidden in this appropriation for the construction of the swimming pool. Repeatedly Senator Stennis asserted that there was no money in the bill for anything associated with the swimming pool. The challenges and denials took up an hour or more of debate time, during which Senator Chavez was seeking recognition, which for some reason was denied him. He finally was recognized and, activating a voice box, for he had had a tracheotomy, advised the Senate that the money for the swimming pool had been included in a bill that he had managed through the Senate a few weeks earlier. The day was carried and the swimming pool was built. The economizers lost that day, but may have found some satisfaction in the fact that because the rule of seniority was observed in the Senate gymnasium long after it had been challenged and modified in Senate legislative proceedings, senators did not fully enjoy the Senate gymnasium until twenty years later, when the Republicans got control of the Senate.

The rule of the Senate gymnasium was that the senior member of the Gym Committee had the right to set the temperature of the swimming pool. The chairman when the pool was completed in the sixties was Senator Willis Robertson of Virginia. Willis liked cool water and set the temperature in the low sixties. Only a few hardy senators from northern states, like Maine, New Hampshire, Washington State, and Minnesota, regularly used the pool. Relief was anticipated following Senator Robertson's defeat. But he was succeeded as chairman by Senator Henry Jackson of Washington State. Jackson, accustomed to the cold waters of Puget Sound, held to the low temperature of Robertson.

Sometime early in the eighties, following the death of

Senator Jackson and the succession of the Republicans to control of the Senate, I visited the Senate gym after long absence. As I approached the pool area, I heard joyful laughter and much splashing. In the pool were seven or eight senators, none of whom had turned blue. I asked the manager of the gym for an explanation. "Warm water," he said. Actually, it was more than warm, it was hot, in the eighties. The old small pool had been maintained for the minority that believed in cold water. There, I observed, seniority, in its last holdout, had been beaten down and had died. Those who remembered Dennis Chavez blessed him.

A senior member of the two committees on which I served in my early years in the Senate was Robert Kerr of Oklahoma. Kerr was an oilman of the original mold, president of Kerr-McGee Oil Company. His commitment was to power, economic and political, although he probably would have quickly traded the economic power for more political power. He did make a try for the Democratic nomination in 1952. In the Senate he played every issue to the hilt. He was one of those people who played for every point with the same intensity, with no regard for the limits of the game. He was quick to acknowledge that he represented the oil industry— obviously a principal concern of his state—as other senators might represent the dairy industry.

Kerr never went so far as to endorse the statement made by once-president of General Motors and subsequently Secretary of Defense Charlie Wilson—"What is good for General Motors is good for the country, and vice versa"—as applying to the oil industry, or more immediately to Kerr-McGee, but he often acted as though he did believe it. He was harsh in debate. One day, after a particularly rough exchange with another senator, he said to me, "I would be better off if I were more restrained. I know that I approach every debate here, no matter how important or unimportant, as I believe a heavyweight boxing champion must approach a fight. If the opponent isn't qualified, he ought not to be in the ring, or in the Senate." He was sharp in his defenses. One day during the Eisenhower administration, while arguing on a tax bill on the Senate floor, he asserted that the President had no "fiscal brains." Republicans were quick to challenge and to demand that he lose his right to speak on the issue, that he be "taken down." They had no solid case against him, since rules restraining speech apply only to what is said about another senator, not about presidents. Nonetheless, the presiding officer stopped debate to hear the case. Kerr sat down for a few minutes and then rose, asking for the floor so that he might apologize. He had, he said, concluded that he had been unfair and wrong. He recalled that in all of the years of Franklin Roosevelt's presidency, Republicans had not, insofar as he knew, made any references to President Roosevelt's physical disabilities. Therefore, Kerr concluded, he would not again make reference to Eisenhower's mental state or qualifications. The remark ended the case but made Kerr few friends.

After Congress amended the tax laws to provide depreciation allowances on cattle breeding stock, he almost immediately bought a herd of purebred Angus cattle. Challenged about his action on a national television show, he first corrected the interviewer, who said that he had heard that Kerr had paid $500,000 for the herd, by saying that he had paid $750,000, and added that once the law was passed, no one in his financial situation could afford not to own thoroughbred cattle breeding stock.

His principal interests, in addition to oil and power, were

conservation and the Baptist church of Oklahoma. He was against alcohol but was heavy into ice cream. I spent two days campaigning with or for him in Oklahoma one year, appearing before labor groups to explain why we had both voted for the Landrum-Griffin Bill. Senators with prolabor voting records, such as I had, were not criticized for supporting the bill, whereas senators who had antilabor records or mixed records, such as Kerr held, were likely to be criticized. A joint appearance, he thought, would eliminate the distinction from his campaign. I spoke to conservation groups, reminding them—if they needed reminding—of Senator Kerr's dedication to the cause of conservation. Between political stops, he regularly questioned his driver as to where the next Dairy Queen or Frostie stand might be.

Kerr's great scourge on the Finance Committee was Paul Douglas of Illinois. Paul would shake his head in disbelief at Kerr's open advocacy of tax policy directly beneficial to the oil industry and to Kerr. The tension between the two was fundamental, Paul's approach to most problems being essentially moral and academic, whereas Kerr's was political and pragmatic. On at least one occasion in a committee meeting they came close to blows after Paul challenged the integrity of Kerr's position. My sympathy was generally with Douglas, who was unique as a senator in a number of ways. He was a most literate man, reflective, wise, highly emotional, a man of deep personal commitment, as manifested in his support of Estes Kefauver for the presidency in opposition to Adlai Stevenson.

Douglas's great political example was John Altgeld, the Illinois politician and governor of the state in the late nineteenth century. Altgeld died in 1902 and was memorialized in a poem by Vachel Lindsay entitled, "The Eagle that is Forgotten." The poem included these lines:

'We have buried him now,' thought his foes,
and in secret rejoiced.
They made a brave show of their mourning,
their hatred unvoiced. . . .

The others that mourned you in silence and
terror and truth,
The widow bereft of her crust, and the boy
without youth,
The mocked and scorned and the wounded,
the lame and the poor
That should have remembered forever . . .
remember no more.

and concluded thus:

To live in mankind is far more than to live
in a name,
To live in mankind, far, far more . . . than to
live in a name.

Paul, more than any politician, honored the name of Altgeld, and did his best to keep the name and the record a living one. This memory may have prompted him, following the death of a contemporary politician, to quote a French philosopher, who had observed that "the death of every animal is a tragedy." "So, too," Paul said, "is the death of a politician."

Paul was one of the two senators I asked to come to Minnesota and speak for me when I left the House of Representatives and ran for the Senate. The other was Wayne Morse. I asked these two because I knew that neither accepted the "club" idea of the Senate, and shunned the attractive "inner ring," which C. S. Lewis said is not necessarily evil in itself, "but which is most skillful in making a man who is not yet a very bad man do very bad things." Both were quite willing to challenge the inner ring of the Senate and to breach the unwritten rule of not campaigning against an incumbent senator.

An annual event in the Senate (though he may have missed a year occasionally) was Paul's speech against waste in government. He evidently kept watch, or someone on his staff did, until he had an adequate list for attack. It may have been his one gesture to the *Chicago Tribune's* antigovernment, antispending position. One year, among the projects he challenged was a study of the "psychometrics of beagle brains." He was critical of the study. I was intrigued by the title and checked out the study to learn that beagle brains were used in brain research and experimentation because among higher mammals the beagle brain comes closest to being standardized. In other words, every beagle brain is very much like every other beagle brain. The choice of a superior beagle among beagles is very difficult because the ideal beagle is the one that is most like other beagles. An outstanding beagle by this standard would not be outstanding. President Johnson had a pair of beagles with him at the White House.

My last exchange, a remote one, with Senator Douglas was over the war in Vietnam. Douglas was no longer in the

Senate and had already written, or was in the process of writing, his memoirs. He had been a conscientious objector in World War I, but had enlisted in the marines to fight and be wounded in action during World War II. He was a strong supporter of our involvement in Vietnam, and when interviewed over my opposition to the war, observed that it took more to be president of the United States than the ability to lead hippies. I thought it a harsh judgment and never sought an explanation from him, but in answer to a press question about his remarks I said that I thought that any ex-senator who had written his memoirs should not be consulted on any current subject. I had not thought of writing my own memoirs at the time, and may, if this book qualifies as a "memoir," be trapped by my own earlier judgment.

Paul was a good man and a good senator, and unless some other senator was hiding his literacy and learning, he was the most literate and learned man in the Senate.

In addition to his militarism and frugality, Paul was highly moral. He was continuously concerned about ethical behavior in Congress, particularly in relation to the possible corruption through the influence of financial or economic interests. He anticipated the rise of Common Cause and would have approved the organization's assertion that "Money is the root of all evil, or at least, of all political evil."

Paul held that the acceptable level of gifts, or payoffs, should be no more than one could eat or drink in twenty-four hours. The rule inherently encouraged alcoholism and gluttony, both transgressions in the range of the lower capital sins, which continue upward through envy, anger, lust, and covetousness to the ultimate sin of pride, with only sloth rated lower than gluttony. Reformers have never given sufficient attention to sloth as a threat to the public good, hence it generally goes unnoticed and unattended, although it may, in fact, have more serious consequences for the commonweal than the other vices and failings that garner more attention.

Over the years, as I have read of payoffs or bribes being offered to members of Congress, I have often wondered what was missing in my own personality or political career, that I was not at least tempted. An inefficient staff may have helped. My administrative aide during most of my years in the Senate was generally opposed to having a staff that was too efficient or dedicated. His principal rule of operation was: "Never trust an aide who gets to the office before you do and stays after you leave." He was proved right in case after case, as senators were done in or put in jeopardy by staff members. The press would report that the staff person who had acted—gone to Drew Pearson, the press, or simply public—had been very dedicated, regularly getting to the office before the congressman or senator and often working late. This was especially true after the introduction of the Xerox machine and the Wats telephone service.

A second rule that he advocated, though this was not limited to congressional offices and can be applied universally, was, "Do not trust a neighbor who offers to cut your side of the hedge." The wisdom of this rule was questioned by his wife and by others, until it turned out that the neighbor against whom he had levied this rule had, in fact, had a wife killed.

I may have been protected in some measure also by the fact that my Minnesota colleague in the Senate put out the word that "If you want something done (something was not specified), don't go to McCarthy, come to me." My defenses were more positive. One of the rules of the office was never to deal with a lawyer, or a representative of a constituent, unless the person being represented was present. This rule was applied especially in immigration cases. If members of Congress caught in the Abscam operation had had a rule of this kind, they would have been protected from exploitation by the FBI.

The combination of inefficiency and principle was not always a sure defense. And although I had never accepted the Douglas rules as compelling, I found myself in near violation of them on several occasions.

One was the case of the postal clerk, the wife of the postmaster in a Minnesota town numbering two to three hundred persons. The wife was charged with a felony, which she had committed by opening and reading the mail of one person being served by the post office. Why this one person was singled out, I never learned. In any case, her husband appealed to me for help, noting that, among other things, her conviction might destroy the vocation of their son, who was in a seminary preparing to become a priest. I did inquire of the Post Office Department as to what might happen, and was assured that the offending wife-clerk would have to resign but would not be prosecuted. This was in the good days before the Post Office was depoliticized. I then advised the postmaster that this was the way it was to be, and wished him and his family a happy Christmas, as that season was approaching, and a successful fulfillment of his son's vocation.

The Christmas was happy, I was informed, and the vocation safe. But my own Christmas season that year, and that of my family, was a disturbed one. A few days before Christmas, in my absence, the postmaster delivered to my house the largest dressed turkey I had ever seen. We had no place to store it, no deep freeze. The weather was very cold, however, so we left it on the unheated porch. We had only two small children, aged one and three, at the time, and had already planned and procured the makings of the Christmas dinner. The holiday passed, but the great turkey remained on the porch. I suggested having a post-Christmas party in order to consume the turkey, which had begun to take on the character of the Paschal Lamb. My wife informed me that the carcass was too large for the oven. I suggested cutting it up, a proposal that was rejected as unbecoming a turkey. After two or three days, during which time the presence of the turkey began to weigh heavily on the family relationship and the holiday spirit, my wife suggested that we give it to the convent of nuns who ran a hospital for the incurably ill. This seemed like a good idea, but it was one that we should have come to two or three days earlier. During the time of our uncertainty, the weather had warmed, and a question as to the wholesomeness of the turkey arose. A report that a turkey given to the nuns by the congressman had made them ill was more than I wished to risk.

Disposal seemed the only course, but not an easy one. At the time, one of the St. Paul city councilmen controlled the garbage disposal program of the city, an important part of which was his pig-feeding project. The city rules provided that any edible garbage had to be deposited, unwrapped, in special garbage cans, whereas paper containers and inedible garbage were to be placed in separate receptacles. The pros-

pect of having the garbage collectors report that the congressman had thrown away a whole turkey seemed a highly
political risk, as did the fleeting thought that I might sneak
down the alley, after dark, and deposit the turkey's body in
a neighbor's garbage can. The conclusion was that as I would
be driving back to Washington alone (my wife and children
would fly), I would take the remains with me and dispose
of them after I had crossed the Wisconsin border, some
twenty miles from St. Paul. I did, and in an isolated place
along the highway, cast out the body and sped on toward
the nation's capital. The size of the bird and the trouble it
caused moved me to believe that there was more wisdom in
Paul Douglas's rule than I had previously accepted.

Paul's second rule banned the acceptance of dry goods.
The exclusion of dry goods may have been prompted by the
experiences he had observed of other politicians in both the
Truman and Eisenhower administrations. In the Truman administration there was the case of General Harry Vaughan
and a deep freeze, and of Matt Connelly, who was done in
—actually convicted and sent to prison—for accepting a suit
of clothing, not for a favor he had done, but for attempting
to do a political favor. Eisenhower as president did not
commute Connelly's sentence, but suffered in somewhat the
same way when his administrative aide, Sherman Adams,
formerly a governor of New Hampshire, resigned under
pressure when it was discovered that he had accepted as
gifts for political favors an Oriental rug, which his defenders
said he had accepted merely to use, as well as a vicuña coat,
or the material for it.

I do not recall ever having been tempted with dry goods,
although I was given twelve golf balls by a large investment

company for supporting, not singly but as a member of the Ways and Means Committee and the Finance Committee, tax legislation that it favored. I was saved, again providentially, from the corruption of consumption of this gift when, in the early Washington spring, with some snow still on the golf courses, a friend of mine, an avid golfer frustrated by the cold and snowy winter of Minnesota, saw grass between the snow drifts on the Washington golf course and asked if he could use my clubs. He borrowed them as well as the dozen balls, and in his afternoon's play lost every one of the balls in the snow. I never hit a single one of them.

Not covered by Paul Douglas's rules was the gift of livestock, or, in my case, a dog. Possibly I could have upheld Paul's rules by eating the dog within twenty-four hours. It was a boxer puppy, Eric by name, that lived to be thirteen years old and gave me and my family great pleasure. In the 1968 campaign we threatened to bring him into the campaign in response to other dog challenges, but concluded that his dignity was beyond politics. We settled by striking a button for him declaring "Eric for First Dog."

Eric was a gift of gratitude to me from a government employee who was among the first to succumb to the temptation of the Wats line privilege of unlimited long distance calling. It seemed that this woman, originally from Minnesota and employed in a government bureau, could not resist the temptation to use the Wats line to call boxer breeders and exhibitors she knew simply to find out how their dogs had done, whether a bitch had had pups, whether a particular dog had won in a show, and so on. The woman was found out and threatened with whatever threats are made in government bureaucracies. My intervention did something good for her (though I never learned what it was), and so I received Eric.

None of these payoffs was discovered by the press or made public. The only exposure I suffered from was one made by Drew Pearson, who reported that on going to Nevada to speak in a campaign for Howard Canon, I had been given the "Nevada treatment"—taken for a ride in a cruiser on Lake Meade and kept in a sumptuous hotel. I advised Drew that we had cold sandwiches and beer on board the boat, and I wrote to him about the hotel room. It did have a round bed, something Drew had not known, but more singular than that, the bed could be made to vibrate merely by pushing a button.

On leaving Congress, I was slightly disappointed not to be offered, as had been some of my colleagues, a directorship in any Minnesota financial institution, even though I had spent sixteen years on the major financial committees of the House and Senate. Nor was I asked to be a consultant, or even to teach or lecture at the University of Minnesota. I did, however, receive comparable requests and offers from institutions in other states. Overall, I was marginally faithful to Paul Douglas's rules.

There were other senators of special note, such as Clinton Anderson of New Mexico, one of the great legislators in the fundamental sense of writing laws. His achievements included the first comprehensive laws dealing with atomic and nuclear power. He was a leader in the successful effort to stop the appointment of Lewis Strauss in 1959 as secretary of commerce in the Eisenhower administration, an opposition based on his experience with Strauss as chairman of the Atomic Energy Commission.

There were others, too, men and women of stature and commitment. Margaret Smith of Maine was among the first to challenge the tactics of Senator Joseph McCarthy, not rushing in where male senators feared to tread, but moving quietly, where they had failed. There was Senator Fulbright, who had a clear conception of the role of the Senate in foreign policy and who, when consent as a constitutional force was bypassed, turned to advice as the only means of influencing foreign policy. Senator Richard Russell of Georgia, a classical senator, was also a classical victim of his times, since it fell to him to defend segregation and to lead the anti–civil rights movement in the Senate.

John Sherman Cooper, a very gentle and painfully honest person, came to one of the press galleries to apologize for having told a reporter that a committee on which he served had not come to any conclusion on a matter before it, when the committee had, in fact, come to some agreement but had agreed to withhold the publication of the outcome. Cooper wondered if he had a right to sit in judgment on another senator who had gotten into financial trouble when he had no such troubles, partly, he said, because he "had married a woman of wealth."

There were other, less admirable senators, some singularly and personally characterized. There were the amenders—that is, members who offered amendments, many irrelevant or obvious, some disruptive and distracting. The extreme example was a senator proposing to change the punctuation mark on a tax bill from a colon, I recall, to a period. He argued that the colon implied that there was more to come, whereas the period would end it at that point. More than the punctuation was involved—some technical parliamentary point. The amendment was defeated, the telling argument being that possibly all tax measures should end with a colon rather than a period, since there was certainly more to come in the way of taxes, and that, in any case, the legislation was unfinished in its effects until the Internal Revenue Service had finished its interpretation.

Then there were the "if you knew what I know" members, claiming to have special knowledge, usually of military affairs or intelligence activities. Their commanding phrase was "If you knew what I (or we) know, you would agree with us." The stopping response was to ask them how they knew that one did not know what they knew, or that, if one did know what they knew, he would agree with them.

There was the "finish it off" group, with a large representation in those years, of liberal Republicans who were accused of entering political battles just as they were about over, shooting the wounded men on the field, and claiming that they had clinched the victory. In character these were not very different from the dog described in Abraham Lincoln's poem, "The Bear Hunt," an activity modern humane society members would scarcely approve.

Early in the poem Lincoln describes one dog as yelping far behind the pack. The dog arrives on the scene after the bear has been killed, and the argument over who is to get the hide is in full cry. The dog, according to Lincoln, arrives upon the spot,

> With grinning teeth, and up-turned hair—
>   Brim full of spunk and wrath
> He growls, and seizes on the dead bear,
>   And shakes for life and death.

And swells as if his skin would tear,
   And growls and shakes again;
And swears as plain as a dog can swear,
   That he has won the skin.

Conceited whelp! We laugh at thee—
   Nor mind that not a few
Of pompous, two-legged dogs there be,
   Conceited quite as you.

Another group in the Senate were the self-conscious or professionally conscious lawyers, distinguished by their disposition in debate or argument to preface their remarks with, "speaking as a lawyer," or, "thinking as a lawyer," as though this condition gave special weight to what they might have to say. Occasionally, I would question one of the lawyer speakers as to how I, a nonlawyer, should interpret his remarks. Was I to assume that I could not understand what he was about to say, or what he had said, because of my nonlawyer status? Or would he explain, if he could, in nonlegal terms, or nonlawyer terms, what he had said, so that I might better understand his remarks? Or, I might ask how he thought differently as a lawyer than he did when he shifted into his nonlawyer mind, and would he tell me when he made the shift so that I could tune in properly? None of the lawyer members who used this device ever gave me a satisfactory explanation, although while trying one or the other might slip in a few Latin terms like "ad hoc" or "duces tecum" as special marks of distinction.

The disposition to legalism in the Senate was not, and is not, a matter of humorous or minimal passing concern. Excessive legalism is reflected in laws that have been passed, and even in Constitutional amendments. The "War Powers Act," more or less legalized short presidential wars. The Twenty-second Amendment, ratified in 1951, established a two-term limitation on a president. The reason given for the passage of the amendment, as stated in 1947, was "the lack of a positive expression upon the subject of the tenure of the Office of President, and by reason of a well-defined custom which has risen in the past, that no President should have more than two terms in that office, much discussion has resulted on this subject. Hence, it is the purpose of this proposal to submit the question to the people so they, by and through the recognized processes, may express their views upon this question and if they shall so elect, they may . . . set at rest this problem."

The explanation and justification are largely nonsense. There had been no popular concern over this issue. There had not been much discussion except among those who had opposed Roosevelt's third and fourth terms, and also, for most of them, his first and second terms. There was no problem to be set at rest. The amendment was proposed as a way of getting even with Franklin Roosevelt after his death. The bearing of the amendment on the presidency has not yet been tested. Early evidence suggests that it never should have been adopted. There have been indications that presidents have begun to think that they have an obligation to serve a second term, if not a right to do so. The consequence of this attitude is that a president in office is likely to be most careful in the first term to assure his reelection in the second. What a president might do in his terminal second term has not yet been demonstrated, since no president has finished such a term since the amendment was passed. It may well be a prescription for two irresponsible presidential terms, the first because of the overriding concern to be reelected, and the second because a president cannot be held answerable to the electorate. The public, too, may come to accept that a second term should be given to every president.

A second legalistic tinkering with the Constitution was the Twenty-fifth, ratified in 1967 and dealing with presidential disability and succession. The movement for the adoption of the amendment began with congressional reflections prompted by the medical histories of Presidents Kennedy, Eisenhower, and Johnson. The health of Woodrow Wilson and Franklin Roosevelt was added to that consideration.

Two sections of the amendment are particularly dangerous. One of these provides that the president can transmit to the Congress a written declaration that he is unable to discharge the powers and duties of his office. His powers then go over to the vice president, and remain with that office until the president sends another letter to Congress saying that he is ready to resume the duties of office. The provision is faulty on two points: one procedural, in that it puts pressure on a president who is partially or temporarily disabled to transfer power to a person whom he might not trust, and the other in that it might open the way to political exploitation when considered in light of the two-term limitation on the presidency. A president who is only slightly disabled might disqualify himself several months before the end of his term so his vice president could take over the office and then present himself as an incumbent, experienced candidate for election to the presidency. This is somewhat the manner in which Nelson Rockefeller resigned as governor of New York well before his current term had ended, without political cause, and allowed his lieutenant governor to take over and then run as an incumbent.

The amendment should at least have made provision for congressional determination as to whether the president is in fact unable to discharge the duties of his office, or as to whether he should be allowed to resign for reasons of health solely by his own determination.

Another section of the amendment is even more legalistic, confusing, and potentially dangerous. It prescribes a complicated procedure whereby the vice president and a majority of the principal officers of the executive departments, or of a body chosen by the two houses, may transmit to Congress their written declaration that the president is unable to discharge the powers and duties of his office, at which point the vice president shall become acting president.

Thereafter, the president can transmit to Congress his written declaration that no inability exists and he shall resume the office unless the vice president and the majority of the previously described body of officers transmit to Congress within four days a contrary declaration that the president is unable to discharge the powers and the duties of his office. Thereupon, the Congress shall decide the issue, having assembled within forty-eight hours if not already in session. Within twenty-one days after receipt of the last declaration, Congress shall act. If by two-thirds vote of both houses it is determined that the president is unable to discharge the powers and duties of the office, the vice president shall continue to carry out the duties. If the vote is less than two-thirds, the president shall resume the powers and duties of his office.

The evidence of lawyer-influence in legislation or in Constitutional amendments is particularly noticeable in its limits on time—thirty days after signing, forty-eight hours after receiving notice, four days, not counting Sundays, and so forth. The possibilities for confusion and mischief in this amendment are almost beyond imagination. A president fit to exercise the duties of his office could be made the target of an ambitious vice president in a kind of palace revolution. A deposed president could, according to the amendment, ask Congress to reinstate him, thus repeatedly triggering the twenty-one day rule for congressional action. The presidency could become like the papacy during the Avignon captivity, or like the crown of England during the War of the Roses. A president under such attack might turn to' the army, navy, or the air force, depending on the kind of pressure he was under. The Republic might have to be saved by the Senate, as Rome, according to historical testimony, was preserved in critical times over the centuries during which the Empire survived.

I may have been prejudiced against lawyer members of Congress, having run against one or two and having been threatened politically by a few others, and also because my own professional background was academic, principally in the liberal arts. Good lawyers, I asserted in campaigns, can be found in the yellow pages of the telephone books. Good historians, or political and social philosophers, are not so easily found or classified.

Hubert Humphrey

In 1948 Hubert Humphrey was elected to the United States Senate representing the state of Minnesota. I was elected to the House of Representatives in the same year. I first met Hubert when he was mayor of Minneapolis, hosting a city hall meeting to organize the Americans for Democratic Action in Minnesota. This was preliminary to the efforts in 1947 and 1948 of Humphrey and others to gain effective control over the Democratic Farmer Labor party which, although formally and legally a political union, had no measurable success, with the exception of the election of one congressman, in the years since the union had been in operation.

The last time I saw Hubert Humphrey was at the Washington Hilton Hotel shortly before his death. The occasion was a fund-raising dinner for the Hubert Humphrey Institute of Public Affairs at the University of Minnesota. He was being escorted back to his table by President Carter after speaking to the audience of his optimism and continuing belief in democracy in America. We embraced, greeted each other by name—and that was all. I had seen him and talked to him about six weeks earlier in the Democratic cloakroom of the Senate. We had a brief conversation, cut short by a senator who interrupted us to speak to Hubert about something that was under debate. At the time of the interruption, Hubert was reminiscing about former days on the campaign trail and about our days together in the Senate. He said that he wished we might have one more good meeting in Minnesota, like those we had known: "You could give them philosophy and jokes, and I politics and a pep talk. The guest speaker would not even want to come on, and everyone would be happy." He was right. Such a rally would have been more in character and more becoming to Humphrey, and more satisfying to him than the Hilton Hotel dinner conducted by the Las Vegas joke-teller Alan King.

In 1952, at the Democratic convention in Chicago, I nominated Hubert Humphrey as a favorite son candidate for the presidency. In that speech I said, "He is the true proponent of democracy. For him, freedom and equality, human dignity and brotherhood are more than abstractions, subject only to the deliberation of philosophers and the lip service of politicians, but ideals to be realized in a democratic society. Hubert Humphrey does not support or offer a watered-down, bargain basement variety of democracy. His demand is for a measure of dedication and inspired confidence so that, in a democratic system, we can progressively achieve a more perfect society based upon justice and freedom . . ." It was more or less a standard nominating speech, except that what might have been judged as clichés when applied to some candidates genuinely applied to Hubert Humphrey.

Hubert wanted to be president, not because of excessive ambition, but because he genuinely believed in politics and in government and in his calling to it. He had a sense of mission, almost a vocation. To be effective politically, he believed he had to be in office, and to be most effective one had to be in the most important office, the most powerful one, the presidency.

He did not spurn lesser offices. After his vice presidency and his 1968 presidential bid, he returned to the Senate. If that opportunity had not existed, he would have been willing, even eager, I believe, to hold a lesser office, perhaps even to become mayor of Minneapolis again.

Hubert Humphrey was forgiving to a fault. At the 1956 Democratic convention, when one of his old political companions and supporters endorsed Estes Kefauver over Humphrey for the vice presidential nomination, Humphrey was doubly hurt and distressed by the action of a man whom he had considered both a friend and a political ally. But when one of his supporters mentioned the word *betrayal,* Humphrey denied that such was the case. "No," he said, "I could see in his eyes when he said he was for me, that he really wasn't." And I said to him, "I don't care whether you are angry at him or not, feel betrayed or not. But why don't you at least pretend for a while that you are, and the next time he calls you to address his organization, suggest that he get Estes Kefauver to entertain the troops." He did not follow my suggestion.

Humphrey's legislative record was a solid one, but his special and distinctive gift was his ability as an advocate—he was an orator. This power was demonstrated most notably in his civil rights speech at the Philadelphia Democratic party convention in 1948, a speech that set the Democratic party on a course that brought it, despite delays and distractions, to the passage of the Civil Rights Act of 1964. It was ironic that Humphrey, who was an advocate of civil rights —the most divisive issue in the Democratic party in nearly one hundred years—was the advocate of unity on the Vietnam War issue in 1968.

Humphrey and others joke about his long speeches. He did give long speeches. I recall having gone to a town in far northwestern Minnesota, near the Canadian border, to give a speech. I spoke for about forty-five minutes, rather a long speech I thought, only to have a number of farmers complain to me for not having spoken longer. Hubert, they said, speaks for at least an hour whenever he comes here. It was not that he liked giving long speeches, and not just that he had a lot to say—although this did figure in determining the length of a speech; it was something more basic. Hubert liked words and language. In speech he was something like a jazz trumpet player. He would go along rather quietly, with little inspiration, then inspiration would come. What he would then say sometimes surprised even Hubert. For example, during the Eisenhower administration in the early fifties, Senator Humphrey was being very restrained. He was being most considerate of the President and the Republicans. The press began to write about the "new Humphrey." And then, in the midst of a structured and contained speech, he took off. "Ike," he said, "is a bird in a gilded cage—kept by the Republicans in the parlor, where he sings sweet songs to all who pass by the window, while back in the kitchen, the Republican blackbirds are eating up the public pie." The speech went on from there to even greater heights (or depths), with references to the creeping, pale, crawling things that grow in the darkness of the Republican basement. Subsequently, I asked him what had happened to the new Humphrey. He said something like, "How about that? I just heard the whistle blow."

In a way his gift for language was a political handicap. In American politics, possibly in democratic politics everywhere, one can say rather extreme, even radical things, if one says them in such a way that people don't remember what one said or who said them. In Humphrey's case what was said was remembered, and it was also remembered that he had said them.

Sticking with adjectives or an occasional adverb as a mark on one's language is a much safer way for politicians to speak than going with statements like this one from Humphrey's civil rights speech: "The time has arrived for the Democratic party to get out of the shadow of states' rights and walk forthrightly into the bright sunshine of human rights." Clear language and metaphor in politics is dangerous.

Hubert always seemed to like what he was doing. His affection for his family was well known. He always spoke glowingly of his father and of the family drugstore back in Huron, South Dakota, to the point that one sensed that he came close to envying his brother Ralph, who ran the store, dispensing pills and encouragement, talking politics and philosophy. Being a druggist, Hubert thought, was good work, and Huron was a good town.

He loved his home on Lake Waverly in Minnesota. Lake Waverly is a very minor lake named after the town of Waverly. One can get a rough measure of a lake and town by the manner of the naming. If the town is named after the lake, it usually indicates that the lake is a good one. If the lake is named after the town, the quality of the lake is usually questionable. Lake Waverly was less than the town, but by a narrow margin. Nonetheless, Humphrey loved the lake, saw the best in it, and talked only of its positive qualities. It held water, it would float a boat, it froze over in the winter, one could skate on it, it had some fish, and it was blue for a few months before it turned green. What more could one expect from a lake?

Hubert was loyal to his friends, to those who helped him, and even to those who hurt him. When he was sworn in as vice president, the person who held the Bible for him was not a distinguished judge, or a clergyman, or a politician, or even his wife, but his most loyal friend and supporter, a man whom some called Humphrey's "bag man," the all but anonymous Freddie Gates. In speaking of Freddie one day, Humphrey said, "You know, we have many friends and supporters who say, 'What can I do for you?' And when you ask they make excuses. Not so Freddie. He does the things you need done." Freddie, a Maronite Catholic, died of a heart attack. His funeral was well attended by both the best of Minneapolis society and the marginal, for he had crossed the borders in the night for both kinds. At brunch after the funeral, just as everyone was settling down to eat, the word came. "They have blown Freddie's safe" (no one knew who "they" were). "They" had, and the contents were never discovered, or if discovered, never made public.

Two elements of Humphrey's life are consistently noted as tragic by his biographers: his financial troubles and his failure to be elected president.

Humphrey's financial troubles were not very different from those of many other politicians of his age and time. This is especially true of those who came into politics immediately after World War II, without private fortunes, inherited money, or patrons. His problems were common to most people coming into adulthood in the Depression and post-Depression years. They continued through most of his political life and ended only in the years after his 1968 defeat for the presidency. Running for the presidency even in the time of less costly politics of the 1950s and 1960s was expensive. Humphrey had no personal fortune or wealthy relatives to draw from and only a few people who might be called large or reliable contributors. Much of his support was sparse and marginal, and often demanding.

He summarized his feelings about his fiscal dependency one day when he was showing me his new house on Lake Waverly. This was before he had become vice president. First he told me that the house was a copy of Lyndon Johnson's guest house. I accepted this, never having been in Lyndon's guest house myself. Then, as we were moving through the kitchen, he paused suddenly and said, "Do you know what my problem is?" I said that I did not. He continued, "Well, I'll tell you. I've got too damn many friends who can get it for me wholesale." He then went around the kitchen, cataloguing appliances, fixtures, linoleum, noting what he had paid for each wholesale and what he would have paid if he had equipped the room on his own at retail. A refrigerator (this is twenty-five or more years ago) that cost him five hundred dollars wholesale was two hundred dollars more than the one he had planned to buy retail. In each case the wholesale price was higher, obviously for better appliances and installations than he would have paid at retail, which he had thought was adequate. He had spent much more than he would have originally spent, and also incurred obligations.

So too, in politics, whatever Hubert got straight away on his own—retail, so to speak—he handled well and competently: the office of the mayor of Minneapolis, his seat in the U.S. Senate. What he got, or was led to believe he got, "wholesale," both the vice presidency, or at least the nomination, and the Democratic nomination for the presidency in 1968 from Lyndon Johnson, proved to be bad bargains. He gave too much and got too little.

His not being elected to the presidency was just short of tragedy. But this and other disappointing elements of his career were largely offset by his successes and achievements. The energy and time, the spirit that Humphrey gave to speeches, are treated by some of his biographers almost as though Humphrey had been indulging in a bad habit, when in fact it was through these speeches that he may well have made his greatest contribution to the good of the commonwealth.

During the years from 1948 to 1964, when there was little legislative progress in the field of civil rights, he was on the speaking trail, giving hope to victims of discrimination, encouraging their leaders to action, and challenging politicians in power or seeking power to act. He was a favored and willing speaker not just in the cause of civil rights, but of Israel, labor, agriculture, and the poor. His proficiency and readiness as a speaker may have hurt his chances for presidential office. He who preaches the crusade may not be called to lead it, at least not to Jerusalem.

Wayne Morse

Of all the members of the Senate, I think Hubert admired and liked Wayne Morse the most. Even when they were in disagreement, he would say affectionately, "Old Wayne, isn't he something?"

I write from the experience of some thirty years of observing Wayne Morse. Ten of those years took place before I had even met him; they were followed by some twenty years of companionship and common work in the Congress of the United States—twenty years of friendship.

I will not write of Wayne's stand on the issues, for that is well known, but rather of his conception of and his respect for the Senate.

He was, of course, always the senator from Oregon. But at the same time he was a U.S. senator—truly aware of the function of that body in the operation of this Republic. He knew the Senate had a strong defensive responsibility: to stand against the House of Representatives, when that was necessary, and to lay down a challenge to the courts. The second was a point which worried him a great deal. I thought of him in the summer of 1974 as we anticipated the Supreme Court decision on Watergate—how Wayne Morse, along with great constitutional observers like Alexis de Tocqueville, had said that the ultimate test of democracy in this country might come through the courts. And, of course, he was concerned about the concentration of power in the executive branch.

In order to meet these responsibilities, he rose above partisanship when necessary, even to the point of leaving the Republican party and moving to the Democratic party. But in that party, too, he was always on the verge of defiance and challenge.

Wayne was never a member of "the club," as they say in the Senate. This was not a matter of personality—because anyone who knew Wayne knew what a great companion he could be—but rather a matter of principle, because the Senate was never intended to be a club. I do not know whether he came to this position from reading Plato or from his own reasoning. But Plato, in talking about the guardians of the state, said that they should never become boon companions. And I have tried to follow Wayne's leadership and example in this respect.

His great concern was over the danger of power in our country—power that was properly defined and properly used. But he was particularly concerned about secret power, power that could not be called upon to explain or justify itself.

His integrity was manifest in small things. Wayne would never simply extend his remarks in the *Congressional Record.* Many senators, especially late in the afternoon when there is no audience, speak for a few minutes and then put the rest of the speech in the *Record,* and it appears as though they had given it. But Wayne would never do that. One could go over to the Senate sometimes at five or six o'clock in the afternoon and hear him speak for an hour. Sometimes there were only two or three people in the galleries, sometimes only his wife. But I often thought of how many people over the years who were there late in the afternoon were impressed to hear Senator Morse telling them and the country what he thought they should hear and never making the rather easy compromise, which nearly everyone else in the Senate made, of simply saying, "Well, I'll put it in the *Record* and get it printed and then distribute it the next day."

He served well, also, by relieving tension on the floor of the Senate. One of his practices was to keep a box of licorice in his desk. He rewarded people; I think it was the old schoolmaster in him. He would say, "You have done well today; you can come down and have some licorice." It got to be rather a mark of prestige if you were approved—especially if you were allowed free access to his licorice box. It was more or less the ultimate test if you did not have to ask permission. He would occasionally demand that you replenish his supply, but even that was an indication that he had somehow approved you and accepted you as deserving of his full trust and confidence.

The greatest testimony to him was that as he grew older, young people's confidence and trust in him grew in strength and intensity. I can think of no higher tribute than that. Of course, his belief in younger people—particularly as he talked about his grandchildren—grew with that same strength. It was reciprocal.

Morse was well described in these lines from a poem written by a Welshman named Vernon Watkins. The title is "A True Picture Restored"; the subtitle, "Memories of Dylan Thomas."

> The latest dead, the latest dead,
> How should he have died . . .
>
> And Wales, when shall you have again
> One so true as he,
> Whose hand was on the mountain's heart,
> The rising of the sea,
> And every passing bird that cries
> Above the estuary? . . .
>
> 'My immortality,' he said,
> 'Now matters to my soul
> Less than the deaths of others. . . .'
>
> Let each whose soul is in one place
> Still to that place be true.
> The man I mourn could honour such
> With every breath he drew.
> I never heard him wish to take
> A life from where it grew.
>
> And yet the man I mourn is gone,
> He who could give the rest
> So much to live for till the grave,
> And do it all in jest.
> Hard it must be, beyond this day,
> For even the grass to rest.

Philip Hart

Certainly the physical death of Senator Philip Hart was a tragedy. But so was the political death that he accepted when, long before he became physically ill, he decided not to run again for the Senate of the United States. There on the edge of despair, still professing faith in American democracy, he spoke of the need that he be replaced by someone of more faith; for his own, sustained largely by act of will, had grown too weak.

Philip Hart was a politician. He recognized politics as an honorable, necessary, and difficult vocation. He practiced it not as the "art of the possible," which is wholly inadequate as a definition, but as a discipline of mind and of will, as a profession that should carry the common good beyond what is considered prudent and possible. He knew that politics is not a game to be scored, to be marked by winning and losing, but that it is a continuing challenge.

It was not within the easy range of the obvious and the popular that Philip Hart labored during his years in the Senate. His name is not associated with the easily drafted, often over-simplified, or the popular: not with food-stamp programs, nor the Peace Corps, nor scholarship programs, although he supported all of these. He was called an active legislator, an identification well deserved.

He was properly credited with being the principal author, or certainly a major author and defender, of the Voting Rights Act of 1965, Truth in Lending, Truth in Packaging, and major revisions of the antitrust laws. Each of these was complicated and controversial, calling for patience and master legal craftsmanship. Phil Hart believed that law could provide structure and order in society. His law was not absolutist; rather, it was designed to set limits and guides. He did not seek to be "the conscience of the Senate," as some have described him. His method was not to express moral judgment or indignation, but to make the reasoned and the pragmatic argument. Even when he attempted to remove Senator James Eastland of Mississippi, the president *pro tempore* of the Senate, from the lines of succession to the presidency, he made no case on moral grounds. He simply said that not to change the order of succession was "outrageous" and beyond any reasonable comprehension.

I do not think he would have accepted statements made by some of his colleagues from the Senate that he "cut through every issue to find the truth and then laid the truth out for all to see." He was too modest and too honest to accept any such credit. Rather, his effort was to come close to the truth, to work around it, and, there on the edge, to ask his colleagues (sometimes to urge them, but with hesitation and some expression of doubt on his part) to take the next step. He asked them to take the risk as an act of civil faith that the commitments of the Declaration of Independence could be realized, but only if they were willing to take chances on the side of liberty and trust.

Phil Hart was not indecisive, as some of his critics have said he was. Like Adlai Stevenson, against whom the same charge was made, he refused to give a simple and immediate response to demands for decision when decision was not called for. Rather, he studied and reflected, and when ready he drew the line and marked the threshold. Only then would he say to his Senate colleagues, "This is as far as I can or will take you. You may cross over with me, if you will, or stand back; but as for me, I have made the choice of crossing."

He was, in the judgment of some, late in opposing the war in Vietnam; but when he declared against it, he left those others who were still supporting it with no defense. He was, in the judgment of some and by his own statement, late in coming to any critical conclusion regarding the activities of the CIA and FBI. When the facts were made clear to him, in the hearings of the Senate committee investigation of those two agencies, his judgment was harsh and final.

He may have been late in asking for amnesty for Vietnam draft evaders and resisters, and for the deserters of that war. But when his mind was made up, his dedication to securing amnesty was total, both as a person and as a member of the Senate. He spoke (shortly before his death) of an amnesty bill that he had introduced in the Senate as one unfinished piece of work that he regretted leaving behind. His wife, Jane, spoke for him when, following his death, she received a phone call from President Ford, asking whether there was anything he could do for her. Her answer was that he could "declare amnesty for the Vietnam protestors, draft evaders, and deserters."

Philip Hart was in many ways a man out of his proper time, a man meant to be in the Age of Faith, or at least in the declining years of that age, when men like Thomas More could make their final defense before the civil law, in religious belief. Philip Hart spoke seriously of God, of heaven, and of religious obligations as they bore upon his private life and upon political action. "Would there be segregation in heaven?" he asked in a Senate hearing. "What of our obligation to practice as a society the corporal works of mercy?"

He could have said without hypocrisy or apology, as Thomas More said just before his death, that he had been in all things the king's good servant, but God's good servant first. Philip Hart was the good servant of his own time—of his family, of his country, of its laws, and of its political institutions, especially of the Senate. But in all of these, because of his own compelling religious beliefs, he was God's good servant first. He was not only pleasing to God; he also met the sometimes more difficult test of being pleasing to man.

While he was ill, I read to him from the Gaelic poet, Antoine Raftery, these lines about the plains of Mayo:

> After Christmas, I will go to the sharp-edged little hill; for it is a fine place without fog falling: a blessed place that the sun shines on, and the wind doesn't rise there or anything of the sort. . . . The lamb and the sheep are there; the cow and the calf are there, fine lands are there without bog. There are oats and flax and large-eared barley. There are valleys with good growth in them and hay. Rods grow there and bushes and tufts; white fields are there and respect for trees; shade and shelter from wind and rain; priests and friars reading their books; spending and getting is there, and nothing scarce. And if I were standing in the middle of my people, age would go from me, and I would be young again.

He asked to hold the book and touched the inscription in it, written by the daughter of William Butler Yeats.

PART III

**A VIEW OF TWO DECADES
(1948–1968)
THROUGH PRESIDENTIAL POLITICS**

MY FIRST INVOLVEMENT in presidential politics—at least as a peripheral experience—was in 1948. In Minnesota, Americans for Democratic Action moved to support the national organization's effort to replace President Truman as the Democratic candidate with Dwight Eisenhower and/or William Douglas. The effort carried as far as the state convention but did not survive it. I was a member, actually an officer, of the Minnesota ADA, but I did not support the effort; I was behind the more regular Democratic Farmer Labor party members who were for the Truman ticket. Not that my support made much difference, but the other effort, even though I was an inexperienced politician, seemed to me an exercise in folly.

The justifications given for opposing Truman were two: his Kansas City background, troubling to reform-minded liberals, and an unsubstantiated charge that he was not a liberal. Whatever doubts and reservations I may have had about President Truman were dispelled when he came into Minnesota on his way back East after what was reported as a disastrous effort in the West, illustrated by photographs of huge stadiums and halls all but empty as Truman made his speeches.

Truman's first stop was Duluth, Minnesota, a city of about one hundred thousand people. The Minnesota party was apprehensive, intimidated by the reports of the Western swing. It was estimated that more than one hundred thousand people were in the streets to greet the President as he rode into the city. Reporters, when asked to explain the throngs as contrasted with what had been reported in other cities, had no explanation except to say that they had seen nothing like them.

A similar reception with numbers estimated at two to three hundred thousand people awaited the President in Minneapolis and St. Paul. Truman's main speech was in the best "give 'em hell" spirit. There were few doubters left among the party members. One of the larger contributors to the party was so encouraged that he gave or lent the Truman campaign enough to get out of town and on to Detroit, and to finance the radio broadcast of the Labor Day speech in that city.

I especially enjoyed Truman's victory and the headline incident in which he was declared the loser. I had had a similar experience with the St. Paul paper in my primary election a few months earlier when the early edition of the paper hastened, before the count was over, to announce my defeat.

Running in the 1948 campaign and subsequently serving in the Congress during the Truman administration was a particularly fortunate experience. The campaign was one in which the presidential candidate and the congressional candidates ran on the party platform, which included the civil rights commitment of the party. Extreme anti–civil rights candidates could support Strom Thurmond for the presidency, and those unhappy or uncertain of Truman's liberal positions had the Henry Wallace candidacy to support. The presidential victory and the congressional victories were tied to the party positions on the issues and made those issues the program for the subsequent Congress.

The Truman Years

The administration established by Truman was a party-based one, the last for the Democratic party, but it was also one that reflected President Truman's sensitivity to the constitutional functions, not only of the presidency, but also of the House, the Senate, and the courts. His was also the last truly constitutional presidency.

Truman did not fit well into the definition of a "strong president" as that definition has been applied by commentators and historians of this century. There had been presidents in our earlier history who were labeled "strong" or "weak," but strength, when it was the mark of an administration, referred more to immediate demands and responses, as in the case of Abraham Lincoln during the Civil War, than to the concept of that office. It was not accompanied by the personalization of the office or by deconstitutionalization, which has marked some administrations.

Of our recent presidents, Harry Truman had the purest concept of responsibility to the office and to the people. He seemed always to know when he was President and when he was Harry Truman. He never cared, or never acted as though he cared, what history might say about him, but rather what it might say about the country. This position contrasts with those of Presidents Johnson and Nixon, who each stated that he would not be the first to lose a war.

Truman openly challenged General Douglas MacArthur, a popular and politically dangerous general, and removed him from his command in the Korean War. Following that, he allowed the general full freedom to express his political views. He did say later, after his presidency was over, that he had made only two serious mistakes as President. One was the appointment of Tom Clark to the Supreme Court, and the other was not firing MacArthur a year earlier than he had.

He maintained a proper relationship with cabinet members. There was no nonsensical talk, during his administration, about being his own secretary of state, for example. And there was little talk about insiders. No one adviser had special status or could claim to be the "inside man," as was to be the case with persons like Walt Rostow, Henry Kissinger, and Zbigniew Brzezinski under later presidents.

President Truman's relationship to the office of president, too, was traditional. There was no talk of giving new meaning to it, nor to the office of the Vice President Alben Barkley, who seemed to be content with the old meaning of the office, best stated by Thomas Jefferson, who saw the vice presidency as a position that gave him time in winter to reflect on philosophy and in the summer to study nature. Although quiet and uncomplaining as vice president, Barkley, it turned out, was not without ambition for the presidency. In 1952 he initiated a campaign for that office. Rejecting the charge that he was too old, he all but ran up the ramp to the speaker's podium at the Chicago convention of that year, and in his speech emphasized the fact that he was speaking without notes or written text, in contrast with some of the younger speakers at the convention. The cynical observed that his eyesight was so poor that he would have been unable to read notes in any case.

Truman maintained a constitutionally defined relationship with the Congress, the House of Representatives, and especially with the House Ways and Means Committee and the Appropriations Committee. He worked closely with the Senate Foreign Relations Committee and emphasized the bipartisan character of the policies of that committee and of its leadership under Republican Senator Arthur Vandenberg and Democratic Chairman Tom Connally. Senators and, through them, the Senate were intimately and responsibly involved not just in the approval of organizations and programs such as the United Nations, the United Nations Relief and Rehabilitation Administration, the Greek Turkish aid program, and the Marshall Plan, but in their development as well. It was the Republican Vandenberg's resolution, adopted on June 11, 1948, that allowed the Truman administration to move ahead with confidence in the negotiations leading to the North Atlantic Treaty. None could make the common complaint of later senators that they are not called in at take-off time, but only for the crash landings. Dean Acheson wrote that the Vandenberg resolution had made the North Atlantic Treaty possible. Said Acheson, "All too often the executive, having sweated through the compromises of a difficult negotiation, laid the resulting treaty before a quite detached, uninformed, and unresponsive Senate, in which a minority could reject the executive's agreement. On this occasion, Senator Vandenberg took seriously and responsibly the word *advice* in the constitutional phrase giving the president power to enter into treaties, 'with the advice and consent of the Senate.' By getting the Senate to give advice in advance of negotiation he got it to accept responsibility in advance of giving consent to ratification."

Truman did not use prior involvement of the Senate as a device for avoiding responsibility that properly belonged to him. According to Dean Acheson, it was proposed to the President at the time of the Korean War that a resolution of support be put through Congress so as to lessen the possibility of criticism. Truman rejected the proposition, saying that what he was doing was clearly his responsibility and that he would proceed, leaving the House and Senate free to criticize if they should wish.

Administrations immediately following Truman had quick and frequent recourse to the resolution. Under President Eisenhower, Congress passed resolutions on Taiwan (1955) and the Middle East (1957), under President Kennedy on Berlin (1962) and Cuba (1962), and under President Johnson on Southeast Asia (Tonkin Gulf, 1964). Some of these resolutions related to areas in which American interests and policies had already been established, such as Taiwan and Berlin, and did little more than say that the president could be president. Others opened the door to significant expansion of American involvement, with the power of Congress and especially of the Senate to give "advice and consent" seriously inhibited. The Middle East resolution of 1957 is an example. It allowed a significant expansion of American commitment in the Middle East through presidential response to requests from existing governments. This became known as the "Eisenhower Doctrine," a variation of which, known as the "Brezhnev Doctrine," was used to justify the recent and continuing Russian invasion of Afghanistan. In a similar manner the Tonkin Gulf Resolution of 1964, although presented and passed primarily in response to what was said to be an unprovoked attack on United States ships in international waters, was later said to have given the President new and special powers.

When President Truman sought to force greater steel production from the United States steel corporations during the Korean War, he issued an executive order taking them over. That order was taken to the Supreme Court and declared to be beyond the President's power of action. Truman yielded to the Court's decision.

Later presidents in trouble with steel companies did not go the route of court orders and court review, but rather of special "influencing" of steel company officers, negatively through midnight calls from government law enforcement officers, and positively through special invitations to the White House to persuade the officers that price-fixing in the White House was in the national interest, whereas price-fixing in Cleveland or Chicago or Buffalo would be in violation of antitrust regulations. The officers of the steel companies evidently liked the White House treatment and, like the nobles of England in the presence of the king, agreed to certain extralegal proposals.

Possibly the clearest example of Truman's concern for the

separation and sharing of powers under the Constitution and for the separation of some government programs from partisan politics was his handling of the appointment of Warren Austin as ambassador to the United Nations, in contrast with the handling of the appointments to that post by later presidents.

Three things were established by that appointment. One was that the ambassadorship was to be above politics and partisanship. The second was that it was an important post, if a senator was willing to abandon his seat in the Senate to accept the appointment. The third was that the United Nations should be a special concern to the Senate. This ambassadorship as conceived by Truman was different from other ambassadorships. The ambassador to the United Nations was not a simple and direct representative of the United States government or of the president but had a special responsibility to represent the United States consistent with our commitments under the United Nations Charter.

Eisenhower did not quite follow the Truman precedent. He did appoint a former senator, one who had been defeated, however, and one from the Republican party. There was no sacrifice of office on the part of Henry Cabot Lodge of Massachusetts when he accepted the appointment, and he was of the same party as the President. The Senate connection was, however, minimally respected. President Kennedy appointed Adlai Stevenson, who had had no service in the Senate and who was of the same party as the President. He was, of course, a person with some political following, even after 1960, but as an appointee was quite clearly the agent of the President. Kennedy raised the office to cabinet status, an action that emphasized the office as being an extension of the administration, weakened whatever lines to the Senate that might have remained, and all but eliminated any independence from administration policies that might be contrary to United Nations Charter obligations. Stevenson remained ambassador to the United Nations when Lyndon Johnson succeeded to the presidency and continued in that post until his death in 1965.

Stevenson was unhappy in the post under both administrations. He told me shortly before he died that he did not intend to accept reappointment when his term ended, if it were offered to him. The Kennedy administration, he said, lied to him, especially about the Bay of Pigs, and Johnson, although he regularly consulted Stevenson, ignored his advice.

President Johnson appointed Arthur Goldberg to succeed Stevenson, asking Goldberg to resign from the Supreme Court to take the ambassadorship. This action completely broke with the tradition of appointing someone with an established political reputation. Arthur Goldberg carried to the office his good reputation and his record of service to the Court. When Goldberg resigned, President Johnson appointed Russell Wiggins to fill out the term. Wiggins was a retired newspaper editor with no political reputation and no association with the Senate. Although the appointment was for a short time, it reduced the office, insofar as appointments are evaluated, to about the same level as that of the Battle Monuments Committee chairmanship.

President Nixon offered me the appointment in 1969. I wanted to take the office, since I saw an opportunity to return the office to what it had been conceived to be and to what it was under the Austin appointment by President

Truman. However, I set as a condition to my accepting it the appointment of a Democrat as my successor in the United States Senate. Having been elected by the Democratic Farmer Labor party, I did not feel that I had a right to give up the office to a Republican. The Republican governor of the state refused to make any such assignment or agreement, and so I rejected the offer.

President Nixon then appointed a career diplomat, Charles Yost, who later was replaced by a newspaper-television correspondent, John Scali, who had neither political background or support nor a definable relationship to the Senate. At various times the office was filled by people like William Scranton and George Bush, both former members of the House of Representatives, and by Patrick Moynihan, later to become senator from New York. Each served well the presidents who appointed him, but none gave the prestige to the office that Warren Austin and Adlai Stevenson had, and they left the United Nations as an institution no better defined than it had been when they assumed office.

President Carter appointed a member of the House of Representatives, Andrew Young, and then announced that the United Nations Ambassador would be the point man for the administration's foreign policy, a further personalization of the office and a further removal of the office from Senate concern and from the United Nations Charter obligations, which it was intended should be recognized in the conduct of that office.

Ambassador Young apparently took the point man role seriously and became involved in international diplomacy beyond that of his predecessor, and was asked to resign. President Carter then chose a career man as Young's successor, William McHenry, who served for the rest of the Carter administration.

While the United Nations ambassadorship had passed from the nonpartisanship of the Truman appointment, through the partisanship and neutrality of career appointees, to the personalization of the office as an extension of the presidency, it remained for President Reagan to politicize the office in the ambassadorship of Jeane Kirkpatrick.

Kirkpatrick progressively made the office not a platform for the presentation and defense of national policy but for projecting Republican political views. To attest to this, one of her final acts while still in office was to attend the Republican National Convention to denounce Democratic party policies, all quite unrelated to the United Nations, its charter, and its tradition. This then completed the degradation of the office from what it was conceived to be and what it was during the ambassadorship of Warren Austin.

President Reagan has appointed as his ambassador during his second term a former CIA member. Russia may follow with a former KGB member, as the role of United Nations ambassador becomes completely confused.

THE EISENHOWER CAMPAIGN

As THE 1952 PRESIDENTIAL ELECTION APPROACHED, the Democrats were not only far from optimistic but were defensive and discouraged. The record of the Truman administration had been good, good enough to warrant his renomination and reelection. But the solid achievements—the ending of the

war in Korea (though the peace terms had not been final-
ized), general economic progress, the beginning of the fight
for civil rights legislation, the establishment of the United
Nations and NATO, and the introduction of the Point IV
program for building the economies of backward nations—
were overshadowed by secondary and peripheral considerations. Although the corruption in the Truman administration was minimal—gifts of a deep freezer, a suit of clothes,
a pair of shoes, possibly a hat—the charge that the administration was filled with "five percenters" took hold and was
trumpeted by the press and the Republicans. The Korean
peace negotiations dragged on, as did the memory of the
war. Disappointment that World War II had not really
ended, despite the celebrations of VE Day and VJ Day,
marked the mood of the country.

The charges of infiltration of Communists and subversives in the government continued to be made without any
significant substantiation. The press headlined almost every
new charge by Senator Joseph McCarthy. Democratic senators who might have challenged him took cover, with one
or two exceptions, most notably Senator Lehman of New
York. Into this disordered party, this cacophony of political
voices, came the voice of Adlai Stevenson. His voice was
clear, pure, almost that of an English horn intruding among
saxophones and trombones.

This voice was first heard in his welcoming speech to the
Democrats at the Chicago Convention of 1952, and it carried
the Democratic party, keeping it from despair during the
following eight years of Eisenhower's victory and administration, until the final rejection of Stevenson by the party in
the Los Angeles Convention of 1960.

As the campaign of 1952 progressed, the chances of a

Democratic party victory faded quickly, despite the quality of its candidate. Eisenhower's "If elected, I will go to Korea" gave him full and clear advantage, clouding the more complicated issues of foreign policy.

The 1952 campaign provides one of the best examples of the technique of the crusade in politics. The Eisenhower supporters insisted that if they were not all political "innocents," they were at least politically innocent. They held that they were nonprofessional, unspoiled and unsoiled, pure citizens. Their opponents were denounced as "politicians." For example, Taft's backers argued that the issue of votes of the Texas delegation was one to be settled "politically," but the Eisenhower supporters would not tolerate the use of that word as applicable to their side of the dispute. They cried out that their opponents were, as might be expected of "politicians," attempting to steal the Texas votes. Similarly, pro-Eisenhower Republicans in Georgia were represented as "good" Georgians, and those supporting Taft as "bad." The campaign tactics were successful in winning the nomination for Dwight Eisenhower. Although the campaign was cast from the beginning as a "crusade," once the candidate of the crusaders won the nomination, compromise was called for—as is often the case once crusades have begun.

The immediate need was a vice presidential candidate, one who could satisfy the conservatives of the Republican party who felt denied their candidate in the rejection of Taft. Someone was needed who could do the rough political work in the campaign if that were necessary, and especially who could carry the anti-Communist campaign against the Democrats.

The choice fell on Richard Nixon, who had won the Senate seat for California in a 1950 campaign against Helen Gahagan Douglas. The campaign's major issue was her "softness on Communism," the theme of the times. There were other anti-Communist champions among the Republican senators, most notably Senator Joseph McCarthy of Wisconsin and Senator William Jenner of Indiana, but Nixon was the freshest and most presentable.

The vice presidential candidate ran into a rough going-over early. The largest problem was what was called a "slush fund," a small amount by modern standards (about $18,000) but large in a campaign charging the Democrats with having run a government marked by "cronyism and corruption."

Press concern over the happiness of the vice president became a matter of public discussion during the Eisenhower presidency when the idea of "giving new meaning" to that office was introduced. The new administration, it was reported, was going to give the vice president special assignments and responsibilities never before borne by a vice president.

The extent of the grant of power and responsibility was brought up during a 1960 Eisenhower news conference near the end of his second term. When asked for an example of a major contribution Vice President Nixon had made to his administration, the President replied, "If you gave me a week, I might think of one. I don't remember."

Despite the President's inability to recall the contribution of his vice president, Richard Nixon subsequently as a presidential candidate represented himself as a strong force in the Eisenhower administration, introducing a photograph of himself confronting Nikita Khrushchev—not merely in Khrushchev's own country, but in his very kitchen. There stood Richard in the kitchen waggling his finger, it appeared, at Nikita's nose. Nixon may only have been pointing, for Nikita did not seem intimidated, or even discomfitted, but rather irritated, if not angry. The photograph became a major prop in Nixon's later presidential campaigns. The 1952 campaign demonstrated that de Tocqueville was close to being right in his observation of the appeal of crusade to citizens in a democracy. When in that campaign candidate Stevenson suggested that the morality of public officials reflected the general level of morality in the democracy, his opponent rejected the suggestion and went on to ask whether the individual United States citizen was responsible for the "fall" of China. The answer expected and given was a very positive no.

When in a campaign speech in New York that year Stevenson said, "Only men who confuse themselves with God would dare to pretend in this anguished and bloody era that they know the exact road to the Promised Land," candidate Eisenhower countered with a speech in Montana encouraging the American people to put away uncertainty and hesitation. "Remember your own power," he said, "and be not dismayed, because you can do anything."

Stevenson asked for patience and forbearance, especially in foreign policy. The crusaders shouted that we had had enough of these virtues and raised the question of whether these were really virtues becoming of Americans. One of the crusaders, a member of Congress and a person of some reputation, stated that the root of American failure was that Americans, acting—of course—through the previous Democratic administrations, had tried to "make a settlement or an arrangement with the devil, Communism, instead of spurning him as Christ did when he was tempted." The same theme continued throughout the Eisenhower administration and was restated two years later when the Speaker of the House of Representatives, Joseph Martin, a Republican, told a Lincoln Day Republican meeting that the "future of all religious faith hung" in the balance of the 1954 congressional elections.

Stevenson fought back, describing the state of the world and outlining his vision of peace and his and the Democratic party's proposals, but to no avail. He did "talk sense" to the American people, but few were listening. Harry Truman might have run better against Eisenhower, although there was little likelihood that he could have won. The general would have been harder pressed by Truman, if this response to Stevenson at the National Plowing Contest in Kasson, Minnesota, in 1952 is indicative: Stevenson, riding in a hay wagon through the crowd toward the speaker's platform, heard a voice from the crowd start raising the old Truman battle cry, "Give 'em hell, Harry," but midway through the shout, the speaker hesitated, stopped, and then completed his cry with, "Give 'em, give 'em heck, Adlai."

Stevenson's followers were not dismayed by his defeat, but rather immediately hailed him as the titular head and spokesman of the Democratic party, a double role that he fulfilled until the election of John Kennedy in 1960. Defining the party's role, attempting to purify political ideas and institutions, and protecting the integrity of political language and thought was Stevenson's duty, as is evidenced in one of his last partisan speeches given in May of 1960, when he said:

If freedom is really the organizing principle of our society, then we cannot forget that it is not an illusion, propaganda, or sedatives, but truth alone that makes us free. Under the influence of the politics of sedation and the techniques of salesmanship, I believe that in recent years self-deceit has slackened our grip on reality. We have tended to shirk the difficult truth and accept the easy half-truth. Perhaps it is always that way. As the old humorist Josh Billings used to say, "As scarce as truth is, the supply has always been in excess of the demand."

No power decrees that America shall have all the breaks and soft options. Neither greatness nor even freedom lies that way. So we must surely return to the reality principle, to the bracing, invigorating, upland climate of truth itself.

Stevenson's last public consideration by the Democrats was at the 1960 convention. He had done little in advance of that convention to push his candidacy, discouraged, I think, by the two campaigns against Eisenhower, especially the one in 1956, which lacked the stimulation of the new issues and challenges of the 1952 campaign. Stevenson might have been better off politically in 1960 if he had passed up the nomination in 1956, as Richard Nixon did in 1964 after losing to Kennedy in 1960, to return as a candidate in 1968. Stevenson did not and, so, approached the election of 1960 twice defeated. The most open support for Stevenson was that shown at the pro-Stevenson rally in Washington, sponsored by Senator Carroll of Colorado and Senator Monroney of Oklahoma, two weeks before the

Los Angeles convention of mid-July. I attended the rally. On July 11 in Los Angeles, an attempt was made to bring his candidacy alive. That day I attended a luncheon at which Eleanor Roosevelt spoke and a late night rally at which I spoke in support of the Stevenson candidacy.

On July 12 the Minnesota delegation leaders caucused until six o'clock the next morning on the question of whom to support. Senator Humphrey was undecided, whereas Governor Freeman, who had been endorsed for the vice presidency by the delegation, argued for support of John Kennedy on the first ballot. It had already been announced that he would nominate John Kennedy the next day. At that caucus I announced my support for Stevenson.

Five hours later, at about eleven o'clock in the morning of July 13, I was called by Senator Monroney and asked whether I would nominate Stevenson. I was surprised to have been asked and requested some time to think it over. In about a half hour Adlai called and asked me. I accepted and that evening placed the Stevenson name in nomination. The response in votes was negligible, 79 out of a total of 1,521 convention votes.

The demonstration following the speech and the supporting speech was far more intense and enthusiastic than demonstrations for any of the other nominees of the convention. It was understandable. Those who were strongly for Adlai cheered, of course. Those who had been for him in the past responded to his nomination, not with votes, but with purging cries of approval to make their change of loyalty easier. Finally the voices of those in whatever categories were left cheered as a testimonial to Adlai Stevenson.

And so ended the active political role of Adlai Stevenson, the purest politician of our times, a politician whose politics were marked by three principal characteristics: first, a decent respect for the opinions of mankind in world affairs, in clear tradition of that principle as stated by Thomas Jefferson (Stevenson was probably the only modern politician who could have had an easy conversation with Jefferson); second, a willingness to accept the judgment of the majority; third, an unselfish surrender of his own personal reputation and image for the good of the common effort, or party effort, if in his judgment that surrender might advance the cause of justice, order, and civility or, at worst, prevent regression.

Adlai did not grow in honor and reputation through politics and the party he served. Rather, both were improved by virtue of his service.

He demonstrated early in his career and throughout his public life a high degree of political humility in his indifference to what historians and biographers might say about him.

Stevenson was truly a contemporary politician, although not recognized as such. He was not ahead of his times, or outside them, or above them, as some critics have said. He was contemporary, passing judgment on his own day, expressing that judgment in words that proved his deep concern, and committing himself to the consequence of his judgment.

He was, in Chaucer's words, a worthy knight who from the time he first rode forth, "loved chivalry, truth, honour, generosity, and courtesy."

THE EISENHOWER PRESIDENCY

THE PRESIDENCY OF DWIGHT EISENHOWER, although generally characterized as a passive presidency, was a highly personal one that left its mark, or marks, on the institution. The presidency may be changed through positive actions, through attacks on the office, or through neglect. Eisenhower affected the presidency more by what he didn't do as President and by what he delegated to others, principally his cabinet members.

President Eisenhower's cabinet was made up of Republicans, few of whom had active political experience in public office. Most of the top people were drawn from the worlds of corporate management and finance. The attorney general was a corporate lawyer. The secretary of state was formerly a corporate officer, and the secretary of defense, the former president of General Motors. Two cabinet members had had automobile agencies, one for Cadillac, the other for Chevrolet. John Foster Dulles, the secretary of state, although long involved in foreign policy, was a member of an international law firm.

Understandably, Eisenhower, with no experience in business and finance, delegated responsibility for fiscal and economic government policies to his secretary of the treasury and his economic advisers. In foreign policy, where he had, at least indirectly, some experience, delegation was the rule. Delegation meant reliance on John Foster Dulles. Eisenhower did not do all that Dulles wanted him to do, the most notable example being his refusal to give direct and open military aid to the French by sending bombers during the siege of Dien Bien Phu, nor did he support any action beyond protest during the Hungarian revolt against the Russians. He did, however, send some nine hundred advisers to South Vietnam, land troops in Lebanon under the conditions of the Eisenhower Doctrine, order a limited action in defense of Quemoy, and permit the planning of the invasion of Cuba to proceed, although he never put the plans in motion, leaving them for President Kennedy.

Eisenhower allowed Dulles to speak for the administration, defining our foreign policy as essentially moralistic and ideological, declaring that "neutralism" was immoral, and making threats of "massive retaliation" if our wishes were denied.

In contrast to the limited and historically defined objectives of the previous administration, Dulles's view was unlimited and open-ended. "Our foreign policy," Dulles declared, "can best be expressed by extending to the whole world the words of the Preamble to the Constitution of the United States. We look at the world as a whole," he said. Dulles brought to his office the commitment of his Calvinist background, with a strong drive to covenant all policies and in so doing to attempt to give them both moral and legal substance. He took credit for strengthening NATO, for setting up SEATO (South Eastern Asia Treaty Organization), for effecting United States adherence to the Military Committee of the Baghdad Pact, and for establishing the Mutual Defense Treaties with Korea, Nationalist China, and Japan. Only Latin America and Africa were left free of special treaty arrangements. There were reports of an attempt to set up an African treaty to contain Gamal Nasser (Egypt was then friendly with Russia). Evidently Dulles thought the Monroe Doctrine adequate to justify Latin American intervention. What was not fully covered by the treaties, Dulles attempted to fill in by resolutions of Congress.

Of the Formosa Resolution passed in 1955, Dulles said, greatly overemphasizing its legal and political aspects, "When Formosa was threatened with attack from the Chinese mainland we got the Far East Resolution passed by Congress. This put the Peiping government unmistakenly on notice that if it attacked Formosa, the United States would immediately be in the war."

The State Department was transformed into a kind of established religion, with ideology replacing historical reality as the determinant of policy.

The process of delegation was carried a step beyond Eisenhower's delegation of powers to John Foster Dulles. Dulles's own delegation included his giving, in some cases, powers that he did not have to the Central Intelligence Agency, directed then by Allen Dulles, brother of the secretary of state. The CIA became a major force in executing and formulating foreign policy. There were two particular advantages in such delegation. First, the CIA was more free of congressional intervention and supervision than was the State Department, and second, it was free to use methods that would not otherwise have been allowed the State Department operatives. It enmeshed itself in politics, taking credit for the overthrow of Arbenz in Guatemala and Mossadegh in Iran. It was active during the years of Eisenhower in Laos and Vietnam and helped to plan the Cuban invasion of 1960–61. It was also responsible for the U-2 flights over Russia with the resultant shooting down of the plane of Gary Powers, an incident that seriously interfered with disarmament talks between Russia and the United States. The Korean War had stopped and peace negotiations were in progress during the campaign when Eisenhower announced, "If elected, I will go to Korea." He did.

An agreement was signed early in his administration, the terms of which were such that Harry Truman said, "If I had agreed to such a settlement, there would have been a move to impeach me." He was probably right. Eisenhower, still the great general of World War II in the minds of most Americans, was beyond criticism. With this strength he could have moved to improve relations with the Russians, whose military knew and respected him. He could have moved against the military-industrial complex which had been challenged and forced back, though not destroyed, between the end of World War II and the Korean War, but which, restored by the latter war, rode on and was consolidated as an institutional force in America during the Eisenhower administration.

In his farewell address, President Eisenhower admonished the country of the power and danger of the military-industrial complex then in place. He might have added that it had been established during his presidency.

During those eight years the Democratic party, with Adlai Stevenson its most articulate candidate since Franklin Roosevelt in both the 1952 and 1956 races and later its titular head and principal spokesman, was never able to mount an effective challenge to Eisenhower's presidential policies. The Democratic party did regain control of the House and the Senate in 1954, however, and retained that control throughout the remainder of the Eisenhower administration.

The one positive good resulting from the eight-year term

of Eisenhower was the successful challenge to Senator Joseph McCarthy and the anti-Communism that had influenced American politics and government adversely for some ten years. Although the action against Senator McCarthy was taken by the Senate, it probably would not have been successful without the support of the administration, or, more accurately, its withdrawal of support from the senator's positions. The anti-Communists needed an administration in power that was forced to make difficult decisions as its target. As long as the target was a Democratic administration they had almost a free run. When the administration became Republican, with Dwight Eisenhower as president, the range of their operations was severely restricted and more risky. In desperation, Senator McCarthy finally attacked the Eisenhower Defense Department with the rousing demand for an answer to the question, Who promoted Irving Peress? a military dentist, reputed to have been a Communist.

Had Eisenhower not been limited to two terms by the Twenty-fifth Amendment, he might well, despite his record and providing he wished to serve, have been elected to another term. The application of the amendment in this case, and possibly in the case of Ronald Reagan, is a demonstration of reformers being caught in their own reforms—not President Eisenhower and President Reagan, that is, as neither was involved in seeking the passage of the amendment, but rather some of the same persons who supported both Eisenhower and Reagan.

The mood of the Eisenhower approach to politics, possibly understandable after considering his experience with life and death as commanding general of much of the action of

World War II, is reflected in his wife's statement that the President's prayer just before going to sleep each night was "God, look after the country until I wake," coupled with Elmer Davis's report that the President, after urging all Americans to spend the first Fourth of July of his administration in 1953 as a day of penance and prayer, "caught four fish in the morning, played eighteen holes of golf in the afternoon, and spent the evening playing bridge."

THE KENNEDY PRESIDENCY

MY ASSOCIATIONS WITH JOHN KENNEDY in the Congress were casual, friendly, and occasionally social. I was invited to his fortieth birthday party, given by the Democratic House members from Massachusetts, and to his wedding, and subsequently, at least once, to dinner at his house in Georgetown, as he was beginning to shape his presidential campaign.

Kennedy's interest in the House of Representatives and his impact in that body was minimal, little different from that of other members of the House in their first three or four terms. When I went to the Senate in 1959, John Kennedy had been there one full six-year term. He had been through the 1956 convention attempt to obtain the vice presidential nomination, and, although he had not announced any intention to run for the presidency, he had become a strong and active force in the Senate, especially in the work of the Committee on Labor and Public Welfare. During the years 1959 and 1960 he handled the presentation and debate on three major pieces of committee legislation: one to raise the minimum wage and to extend the coverage of the law and second, a comprehensive education bill in which, with his leadership, an attempt was made to eliminate the loyalty oath requirement for students receiving grants and loans. The attempt was unsuccessful. Senator Kennedy asked me to speak in support of his proposal. The third major bill handled by Kennedy in those years was labeled the Landrum-Griffin Bill, carrying the name of a Democratic member of the House of Representatives, Congressman Landrum of Georgia, and the name of Republican Congressman Griffin of Michigan. It was generally accepted that in handling this legislation John Kennedy had proved his competency, both legislatively and politically. The bill dealt primarily with internal labor union affairs, with accountability of labor union officers, and it had mixed support from the labor movement. Some of the support was defensive, from labor union officers set on proving their dedication to purity and accountability. Some of the support came from labor leaders who were challenging other unions and other labor leaders. It was not easy and was not a comfortable spot for a potential presidential candidate. In the course of the consideration of the legislation, I had the only experience with John Kennedy that disturbed me. I was asked to offer an amendment supported by some members of organized labor and also by civil libertarians who believed in equal protection under the law and in the principle of "innocent until proven guilty."

The amendment provided that a union might give financial support to a union officer indicted under the law in making his legal defense if the charge related to something he had done as an officer of the union. The legislation, as it was presented to the Senate, provided "whereas the union could not provide financing to an accused officer while he was under trial, that if he were acquitted, they could recompense him for what it had cost him to defend himself." I talked to Senator Kennedy about that amendment before I offered it. He said he would support it. Once I offered it, a great storm of opposition arose. Charges were made that with enough money to pay for a defense, labor leaders would not be convicted. This seemed a strange argument to me unless one assumed that money is the condition of justice. One senator shouted that this would cause Jimmy Hoffa of the Teamsters to throw his hat into the air. And so it went.

During the course of these exchanges, Robert Kennedy came onto the floor and talked to Senator John Kennedy, who soon announced that his committee could not accept the amendment. Senator Kennedy subsequently came to my desk on the Senate floor, and said, "I'm sorry about that." I replied that it was all right but took note that I could never accept his more than casual word on a legislative matter again.

The John Kennedy of the Senate, in contrast with the John Kennedy of the House, showed a change comparable to that of Prince Hal in the Shakespearian version of Henry V.

As the 1960 presidential campaign approached, Senator Humphrey and his supporters, undeterred by the vice presidential experience in Chicago four years earlier, began organizing and planning a Humphrey campaign for the Democratic presidential nomination. In 1956, when Adlai Stevenson, as the party nominee for the presidency, threw the choice of a vice presidential candidate open to the convention, Hubert Humphrey became a candidate. In the balloting he finished fourth, a disappointment to him and something of a surprise. Persons like Walter Reuther of the auto workers, a long-time supporter of Humphrey, had supported Estes Kefauver. In the postmortem discussions of the balloting, one of Humphrey's supporters expressed the opinion that Reuther had double-crossed Humphrey. Not so said Humphrey, adding that he knew and that Walter knew, that he had never made a full and first commitment to Humphrey. It was suggested to Humphrey that, even though he did not feel that he had been done in by Reuther, he should act as though he did and refuse the next Reuther invitation to come to Detroit to entertain the troops. It appeared that the 1960 presidential race would be wide open. In the early months of the year and on through the West Virginia primary, Kennedy support appeared to be thin and uncertain. At the midwest Democratic conference, held in Detroit in April of that year while the Wisconsin primary was still in progress, the case for seven possible nominees was presented. Five of the potential nominees were present in person: John Kennedy, Senator Stuart Symington of Missouri, Governor G. Mennen Williams of Michigan, Governor Robert Meyner of New Jersey, and Senator Wayne Morse of Oregon. Speaker of the House of Representatives Sam Rayburn was there to speak for Lyndon Johnson, and I to speak for Hubert Humphrey. I was cochairman of the Humphrey campaign and campaigned for him in the two primaries in which he participated, those of Wisconsin and West Virginia.

The positive case for Humphrey was his dedicated work

in the battles for civil rights, agriculture, and labor legislation. In Wisconsin the only negative issue raised against Kennedy was his voting record on farm legislation. Humphrey lost the Wisconsin primary, but not by an overwhelming or discouraging vote.

Some Humphrey supporters, looking at the Wisconsin returns, concluded that Kennedy had won because of a strong Catholic vote. The evidence was clear that he had received that vote, although it was not established that he had received it because he was Catholic. Humphrey supporters anticipated the test in West Virginia, where the Catholic population is practically nonexistent. They did not raise the religion issue directly, but did not conceal the circumstantial evidence of religious support for Kennedy in Wisconsin. They did raise the issue of family money being spent on the campaign in West Virginia (something which didn't seem to bother West Virginians then or subsequently, as evidenced by their repeated election of Jay Rockefeller to office). West Virginians may have been disarmed by the response attributed to Rose Kennedy who, when asked about the expenditure of family money for political purposes, said that it was their money and they could spend it as they wished.

As the West Virginia campaign progressed, Senator Kennedy called me at the Senate office building, asking whether he could come to see me. I responded that he was busier than I, and that I would come to his office.

After I was seated, he got up from his chair and came around the desk and, standing over me, said, "Tell Hubert to lay off in West Virginia or we will unload on him." I responded that I was not running the Humphrey campaign and I would not carry the message, and suggested that if he wanted that message to get through to Humphrey, he would have to get someone other than me to carry it. I added that I thought he, Kennedy, was doing all right, in any case.

I never checked to find out whether such a message was ever given to Humphrey. Not long after my meeting with Kennedy, Franklin Roosevelt, Jr., arrived in West Virginia, campaigning against Humphrey primarily on Humphrey's draft record in World War II. This was an old issue, repeatedly used against Hubert by his Republican opposition in Minnesota. After his defeat in West Virginia, Humphrey withdrew from the contest for nomination.

With Humphrey out of the race, my participation in the campaign was limited primarily to participating in panels and programs on religion in politics. One of the earliest, held during the Wisconsin primary, included Paul Blanchard, who was at the time the most outspoken opponent of Catholics in politics. After the program, Blanchard took me aside and, with a note of apology for asking the question, inquired as to whether I thought Kennedy might win or lose the Wisconsin primary. The reason for his concern, he said, was that his forthcoming book about the danger of having a Catholic president, which had been scheduled to come out in January, had been delayed and would not be out until June. A Kennedy defeat in Wisconsin, Blanchard noted, would hurt sales. Ideally, it seemed that he wished to have Kennedy run well enough to move people to buy the book and then lose the nomination. Kennedy did win in Wisconsin. I assume book sales were good.

The Minnesota delegation went to the 1960 Democratic convention uninstructed and without a candidate. I went as a member of the delegation, uncommitted to any candidate, having done little more after the primaries than attend a Washington, D.C., rally for Adlai Stevenson, held two weeks before the convention. It was a rally without a candidate, essentially an expression of hope that Adlai might run.

At the opening of the convention I had reservations about the candidacy of Senator Kennedy. I had no positive case against his candidacy, but it was my general opinion that he had not yet proved himself and was less qualified to be president than was Adlai Stevenson. I also had reservations about the candidacy of Senator Johnson.

I was publicly announced, along with Senator Mansfield, to be a supporter of Senator Johnson at a press conference held by Senator Robert Kerr. The announcement was made without my clearance, and somewhat overstated my endorsement of Johnson. I did not repudiate it, but qualified my endorsement by saying that I thought that Senator Johnson would make a better prime minister than a president. As a prime minister, I said, he would be more subject to party determinations, and his capacity, well demonstrated as majority leader of the Senate, for getting as much out of a situation as was in it could be fully tested. I expressed doubt about his ability to move the nation to new and undefined objectives. I am of the opinion that if Lyndon Johnson had come to the presidency through the regular way of first being nominated by his party and then elected, his presidency would have been different, not necessarily "great," but controlled and solid.

Some of the noted observers of American politics in 1960 said that my support and nomination of Adlai Stevenson at that convention was to service the interests of Lyndon Johnson. They were nearly one hundred percent wrong. My support of Johnson, little as it was, was a holding position, primarily in hope that Adlai would become a candidate. During the process of selecting or electing delegates to the 1960 convention, Adlai never publicly stated that he was a candidate, nor did he say anything to me in private to indicate his intentions. He may have stated such to Senators Monroney and Carroll. If he did, they kept his word secret.

At the Los Angeles convention in July of 1960, his candidacy began to come alive. I nominated Stevenson, at his request.

The speech I gave for Stevenson moved some Kennedy supporters and political reporters and commentators to the assertion—if not the belief—that a feud existed between me and John Kennedy. Chester Lewis, Hodgson Godfrey, and Bruce Page, writers of one of the best books on the 1968 campaign, *An American Melodrama,* were moved to speculate on the possible origin of "the quarrel," which had in fact never existed, although I am sure that the speech for Stevenson did not please John Kennedy.

If I had had presidential ambitions as early as 1960, a Kennedy candidacy, and thus a Catholic candidacy, would not have been the most serious obstacle to my own candidacy. Rather, the obstacle would have been the continuing candidacy of Hubert Humphrey, my Senate colleague from Minnesota.

The 1960 convention's choice of the Democratic vice presidential candidate that year was complicated, if not confused. With reasonable certainty that Kennedy was to be nominated, vice presidential hopefuls began to move into position even along the way to the convention and, then, emerged at the convention. There were at least five or six who thought they were under consideration, some because of assumed merits, others for having delivered their delegations to Kennedy. There were several governors: Herschel Loveless of Iowa and George Docking of Kansas, whose delegations did support Kennedy, and Orville Freeman of Minnesota, who placed John Kennedy's name in nomination but could not deliver the votes of the Minnesota delegation. There was Senator Stuart Symington, whom many believed to be the front runner, and Lyndon Johnson, who was mentioned but seemed unresponsive.

The choice of Johnson was surprising, pleasing to some, and bitterly denounced by others whose reaction was demonstrated in the great cry of "No!" from Governor Williams of Michigan when the announcement was made. Johnson, of all the earlier challengers of Kennedy, had carried his presidential cause to the convention, losing by a vote of 806 to 409, out of a total of 1521. According to Johnson staff members, Lyndon was reluctant to accept the vice presidency and was urged not to do so by Robert Kennedy. Johnson reportedly responded to Bobby's assertion that he was not wanted on the ticket, "Tell your brother to say that to me." Evidently Jack Kennedy did not, and, with the urging and advice of Sam Rayburn, Johnson accepted the nomination.

Observers of the campaign and interpreters of the results generally agreed that Johnson's presence on the ticket did help Kennedy to victory in some states, and Johnson went on to an unhappy vice presidency. He did some traveling and attended funerals. He murmured that he felt excluded, politically and socially, from the Kennedy "inner ring," and even secondary rings. President Kennedy is reported to have said, in any case, that every time he consulted Lyndon and did what he recommended, *things did go well,* but when he failed to consult Lyndon or to take his advice, *things worked out badly.*

Johnson, more than any other vice president before or after him, stayed close to the Senate. He did this physically, in holding onto much of the office space he had used as majority leader, and also politically and socially. He was reluctant to give up the power, or the appearance of power, that he held over that body. Evidence of this reluctance was demonstrated soon after Lyndon became vice president.

At the first caucus of the Democratic members of the Senate, the new majority leader, Senator Mansfield, proposed that the vice president be invited to preside over the future caucuses. Whether the idea was Mansfield's or Johnson's, we never learned. In any case, some of the members of the caucus objected. Senator Morse and I were among them and spoke against the idea. Senator Morse emphasized the principle of separation of powers and argued that Johnson was formally and constitutionally a part of the executive branch of the government and should not be included in caucuses that might be concerned with matters in disagreement with the executive branch. I spoke of the parliamentary tradition, even though it had become a formality, of excluding the Speaker of the House from some deliberations on the grounds that in earlier times he had been looked upon as the agent of the king. This practice of exclusion was incorporated in the Rules of the House of Representatives, in the provision that the House might operate with the Speaker denied the chairmanship.

The practice exists for reasons quite different, of course, from those given for the British exclusion; it relates to simplified proceedings and to giving the Speaker relief from the boredom of presiding. There were other incidental considerations, principally the rejection of even the appearance of Johnson's continuing to manage the Senate, even though the caucus was seldom used. The count of votes against was a little unclear, since no formal record of the vote was kept. Estimates set the vote at seventeen against and at least twice that in favor of the Mansfield proposal.

Whether Johnson knew about the proposal before he was offered it, is not known for sure. He was unhappy when he learned that it had been challenged, an indication of his lack of sensitivity to traditional and institutional relationships, which was to show in more serious ways after he became president.

Lyndon was not slow in showing his displeasure. Either the night of the day the vote was taken, or a few nights later, he appeared at a cocktail party given by Agnes Meyer, publisher of the *Washington Post* and the *grand dame* of the city that year. Her invitations were not unlike ultimatums. In this case, the response had been heavy. Lyndon arrived after the party was well in progress. He began working the crowd, but seemed to be in a heavy mood. Eventually (after his wife had left) he found me, near the middle of the drawing room, and moved in on me. As Lyndon pushed his case in harsher and louder tones, guests began to fall back against the walls, like the crowd response in a Western in anticipation of a shootout. One or two persons tentatively ventured forward and then retreated.

He was highly upset over my opposition to the Mansfield

motion and ran off his litany of all that he had done for me, and for others who had voted against him. I was not particularly disturbed and attempted to explain that my position was based on concern for institutions and history, and was not personal. He was heard by many as he said, "I'll take care of you, never fear," to which I responded, "You just do that. But don't do more than get even." It took intervention by my wife to end the confrontation. He withdrew and, putting an arm around my wife's shoulders, said, "Well, anyway, we do love you and Muriel (Senator Humphrey's wife)." I do not know why Mrs. Humphrey was included, for Senator Humphrey had not opposed the inclusion of Lyndon in the caucus. I read it as a sign of his first experience of the frustration of being vice president.

I could not point to anything that he did, either as vice president or subsequently as president, that could be interpreted as "taking care" of me.

Among vice presidencies I have known, I would say that the Johnson vice presidency, apart from the support it gave to John Kennedy in the election campaign, best demonstrated why the office of the vice presidency should be eliminated. It can take a person of great ability, an effective member of the government, especially of the Congress, and place him on the sidelines for four years or more, barring the death or (in the case of Richard Nixon) the resignation of the president. There are simple, workable ways by which a president can be replaced, as was demonstrated in the congressional election of Gerald Ford to the vice presidency when Agnew resigned.

In the campaign of 1960, and in the three years of his administration, President Kennedy gave no indication or evidence of his having any resentment of what I had done in the convention or prior to it. Nor did he give any indication that he felt that he and I were involved in a feud.

Immediately after the convention, the Kennedy campaign asked me to campaign principally with what they thought were disaffected Stevensonian liberals, and also with liberals whom they thought, with some reason, might be basically anti-Catholic. In that campaign, I traveled over 60,000 miles for the Kennedy-Johnson ticket.

When soon after the election I collapsed with pneumonia, John Kennedy, elected but not yet sworn in, came to visit me at the hospital. He was there to visit his wife, who had just delivered a child. He talked of his cabinet and especially about a possible appointment for Governor Freeman. Orville was interested in being attorney general or secretary of defense. Evidently he was not going to be given either of these two posts, since Kennedy inquired as to the possibility of making Freeman head of the Veteran's Bureau. I thought it too little to satisfy the governor. Later I received a call from Governor Freeman, who had come to accept that he was not going to be offered either of the posts he preferred, asking me if I would suggest his name to the president-elect as a possible secretary of agriculture. Senator Humphrey, in the interim during which the governor was waiting to be called to some other post, had committed himself to another candidate for the office of secretary of agriculture. His candidate was a somewhat aged Farmers' Union leader who, it was reported, fell asleep during his interview with Kennedy. I did recommend Freeman, who was named, noting that a senator from a farm state runs a high risk in having someone from his state as secretary of agriculture.

More evidence that John Kennedy had no intention of continuing an alleged feud came soon after his inauguration. In declining the invitation of Robert Riggs, the president of the Gridiron Club, to speak at the annual banquet, Kennedy proposed that I be the respondent for the administration and the Democrats. According to Riggs, the president was pleased with the speech, saying that it "was the most sophisticated political commentary he had ever heard."

Subsequently, I was asked to carry out two diplomatic missions for the President, something no other administration had asked me to do. One was to the Vatican during the Vatican Council meeting of 1962. The mission was to find out whether the Vatican favored a presidential visit and, also, to discuss the Vatican position on U.S. cooperation with what was then called the Italian government's "opening to the left."

The State Department's position at the time was that the U. S. cooperation was not approved by the Vatican. The issue of an ambassador had been raised during the campaign. Kennedy had rejected the possibility of sending one but felt that some relationship with the Vatican and some common understanding would be helpful in carrying out foreign policy. He was also skeptical of the advice on Italian affairs coming from the American embassy in Rome.

I met with Cardinal Cicognani, whom I had known both during his time as papal delegate in Washington and through some associations with him when I was on the faculty of St. John's University. The cardinal said that he did not think it necessary to identify someone in the embassy as an unofficial representative to the Vatican, if the Vatican on its part would designate someone with whom there could be more direct communication. Cicognani said, "This is not a political pope. He thinks political matters should take care of themselves. His concern is for the Church." And on the question of the opening to the left, he said of the pope, with an opening gesture of his hands and arms, "Open to the left. Open to the right. Open."

An audience with the pope followed. He was very interested in John Kennedy and said that he thought Kennedy would do new things, and that there was much that was new in the world. The pope inquired as to the President's health and said that, though he had met a number of the members of the President's family, he had not met the President.

A second mission for the President, requested early in the administration, was that I go to the Third International Christian Democratic Conference held in Santiago, Chile. I knew various leaders of the Christian Democratic parties from Europe and South America, and had read their writings, as some of them had read mine. In preparing to implement the Alliance for Progress, President Kennedy was concerned to know the strength of the possible third force in Latin America and to form some opinion of its leaders.

The United States was well represented in Chile at the time by Ralph Dungan, the ambassador and close friend of the President, and also by the U.S. chargé d'affaires, Minister John Jova. After the conference, and after private meetings with some of the Latin American Christian Democratic leaders, I reported to President Kennedy my confidence in the two most important Christian Democrat leaders in Chile, Eduardo Frei, later to be elected president of that country, and Radomiro Tomic, the second in the line of power in that party, and also in the leaders of the party in Venezuela.

Subsequently, a symposium on Latin America was held at Georgetown University, and Frei and Tomic were invited to speak. The visit included a meeting with President Kennedy and members of the Foreign Relations Committee. Eventually, with some support from the administration, Christian Democrat Frei was elected president of Chile, and Christian Democrat Rafael Caldera, president of Venezuela. It was a good beginning on the "Alliance for Progress."

Apart from the extra-senatorial tasks, the most satisfying senate service for me during the Kennedy administration was that on the Finance Committee. The committee, supported by the administration and by economists such as Walter Heller, challenged the negativism of the conservatives and launched an economic program, the centerpiece of which was tax reduction in the face of an improving economy. This ran counter to the accepted Keynesian doctrine, and full in the face of the conservative economists and their press instruments.

I did not see the President, except through the media, during the critical times of the Cuban invasion and the missile crisis, but did see him occasionally in the White House at bill signings and routine White House conferences. He was easy and relaxed. One day he was about to step out into the Rose Garden to speak to a group of students, Girls' Nation, I recall, when he turned to me and said, "What speeches are you giving now? I'm back to my 1952 file."

He visited Minnesota as President in October of 1962 before the missile crisis had occurred. The occasion was purely political, a fund-raising dinner. Kennedy attended Sunday mass at St. Paul Cathedral. Knowing the habits of the Boston Irish Catholic politicians, he was prepared to deal with the Minnesota variety, limiting those in the pew with him to my wife and me, and excluding the eager politicians whom he suspected of being no more than political church-goers.

Dave Powers was with him that day, and performed well in the hotel room as the President fed him the customary questions about how he had done in some remote precinct of the election. Dave had the figures ready. The President commented, on the motor route from Minneapolis to St. Paul, on the sparseness of the crowds. A mild rain was falling, and the limousine roof leaked slightly. He asked me why I did not have a missal, a proper prayerbook, as we approached the Church. Teddy, he said, "carries one that he can hardly lift with both hands." As was customary, the preacher of the day had been asked to avoid controversial political and even religious issues. The speaker of the day was an auxiliary bishop, the archbishop having already left for Rome and the Second Vatican Council. As the bishop proceeded to tell of the happy condition of the Church, and of how fortunate it was to be having a Council when there were no great divisive issues in the Church, the President began to drum with his fingers on the back of the railing before him and eventually leaned over to me and said, "If the Church is in such good shape, I don't think I would have called a meeting."

I flew back to Washington on the presidential plane. It was a trip during which, according to some of the political experts, the President supposedly already knew of the coming trouble in Cuba. He may have, but if he did, he went to elaborate lengths to disguise that knowledge from those who flew with him from Andrews Air Force Base to the White House in the presidential helicopter. The pressing question was whether he should wear a hat to Danbury, Connecticut, the hat-making capital of the United States.

It was after the President had mastered the missile crisis and was settling into the presidency, in the third year of his administration, that he was assassinated. On November 22, 1963, the day of the assassination, I was at lunch in a restaurant near the Capitol when the word came to me to report to the Senate floor because the President had been shot. The report I received said that the condition was most serious. I stopped for a few minutes in St. Joseph's Church, which was on route from the restaurant to the Capitol, and then went on to the Senate floor. The word there was that the President had been given the last rites of the Church and that he was near death. I returned to my office and sat down to write in what seemed to be anger at Dallas, for I remembered how, not long before, Adlai Stevenson had been spat upon and abused in that city. Eventually, I wrote this testimonial to John Kennedy:

In *Look* magazine in July 1963, Sidney Hyman wrote of trouble on the New Frontier:

A baffling dark breeze is now blowing through Washington's political community. No one knows for sure what whipped it up, why it portends, or when it will pass away. The effects take many forms. There are murmurs of things that are vaguely wrong, of plans to set something vaguely right. But there are no prophets shouting. If any one speaker dominates the Washington scene, it is the professor who shows with charts why it is manly to seek only the possible and not the good—to let the part pass for the whole . . . to make workability the proof of truth and usefulness the test of value.

There were, to be sure, areas of failure in the Kennedy administration by late 1963—and much unfinished business. The overemphasis on armaments and on the missile gap in the campaign of 1960 had set the country on a course of larger and larger military budgets, and perhaps had led to the invasion of Cuba, the subsequent missile confrontation, and the humiliation of Khrushchev, a humiliation which contributed significantly to his fall from power and to the suspension, if not the reversal, of the move to ease East-West tensions.

With the advice and counsel of Dean Rusk, the secretary of state, and of Secretary of Defense Robert McNamara, the President, in committing approximately 16,000 troops to Vietnam, had changed our involvement there in a quantitative way.

Whether he would have escalated the war as did President Johnson, no one will know. Some of his closest associates say that he would not have done so. There is reason to believe that they are correct. President Kennedy did limit American participation in the Cuban venture and ended it without the showdown that some were urging on him. He might have been more responsive to early critics of the war, since most of the critics were closer to him both as persons and as politicians than they were to President Johnson.

The wisdom of the Kennedy administration's economic policies was reflected in rising production, a fall in unemployment, and a reasonably controlled rate of inflation.

The problems of the poor and of the chronically unemployed, however, were not met. Urban decay continued. Progress in civil rights was more a consequence of the execution of court decisions than it was a result of legislation recommended by the President and passed by the Congress. The major legislative record on civil rights was to be made later.

The personalization of the presidency, first as a matter of style and then as to procedures and substance, advanced. Carefulness and compromise in anticipation of the 1964 election more and more became the marks of the administration; the New Frontier became, in some measure, a rear-guard action or holding operation.

But the spirit in America in 1963, the last year of the administration and of the life of John Kennedy, was one of optimism and hope. Quiet courage and civility had become the mark of American government. New programs of promise and dedication—the Peace Corps, the Alliance for Progress—had been presented and to some degree accepted, if not realized.

The promise for equal rights for all had been given, and a beginning toward the fulfillment of that promise had been made. What the continuation and flourishing of the good spirit released in John Kennedy's administration might have done for the nation remains an unanswered question.

LYNDON JOHNSON

THE DAYS AND MONTHS following the assassination and the
burial of President Kennedy were times out of joint. There
was an emptiness, possibly intensified by the brilliance of
the funeral and its dramatic character: the horse-drawn cais-
son, the riderless horse, the boots reversed in the stirrups,
the jets flying over Arlington Cemetery, the Irish rifles, the
grieving widow, the puzzled children.

When President Johnson succeeded to the presidency, he
faced no easy or pleasant task. The first concern seemed to
be to have the assassination explained. Within a week after
the assassination, the President appointed a special commission to investigate and report on it. He and others anticipated that unless a highly trusted group of individuals
was appointed to conduct the inquiry and to publish its
results, public suspicion and uncertainty might last as long
as or longer than they had about the death of Abraham
Lincoln a century earlier.

The Johnson procedure was characteristic of him. He
wanted the work done quickly. He picked persons for the
commission who not only had personal reputations of public and personal integrity, but who also held high and important offices in government. He, it appeared, was willing to
pledge the personal reputations of the committee members
as well as the value of the offices they held in order to
reassure the public and assure acceptance of the report.
What little hope there might have been that an objective,
solid report on people and events leading up to and following the killing was largely dissipated by the killing of Lee

Harvey Oswald by Jack Ruby and by Ruby's subsequent death.

Suspicion and fantasies about the killing of the president were held in abeyance until the filing of the Warren Commission report on September 27, 1964, a little less than a year after the assassination. The report was generally approved by the establishment press, as it too wanted an end to speculation, even to reflection, on the event. A *New York Times* report described the report as "exhaustive," and the evidence as "overwhelming." Along with the report, twenty-six volumes of testimony and evidence were released. Before long, articles and books began to appear questioning the findings of the commission. By 1968, more than twenty different explanations of the assassination were in circulation.

Chief Justice Earl Warren was asked to be chairman of the commission. The chairman was asked to take the status vested in the highest judicial office of the country and place the constitutional and traditional significance of that office behind what might be in the commission's report. Gerald Ford, Republican House Leader, and Hale Boggs were chosen as Republican and Democratic members of the House of Representatives, thus placing the integrity of that body and its leaders on the line for the report. Senator Richard Russell, a Democrat, and Sherman Cooper, a Republican senator, were chosen from the Senate for the same reason. These were supported by John McCloy, a stalwart of the Eastern establishment with a reputation for wisdom and integrity, going back to World War II, and by Allen Dulles, former director of the CIA, evidently chosen to assure the investigation would be thorough.

I asked Senator Russell how he came to be appointed and

why he accepted the appointment to the commission, for I knew of his deep regard for the Senate and for the separation of powers of government. I suspected that he understood why President Johnson was appointing the persons he had nominated for the commission. Russell said that when asked by the President to take the assignment, he had refused and argued, much as I thought he would, against taking it. Finally, President Johnson said, according to Russell, "Well, I am going to name you to the commission tomorrow morning. If you are not going to take the appointment, have your excuses or explanations ready to give to the press after I have named you."

The naming of the commission was a clear demonstration of President Johnson's lack of a sense of the institutional importance of government bodies, of his barbarian (in the classical sense) disposition to subordinate, if not destroy or seriously corrupt, institutions by presidential will, and of his personalization of the office of the presidency.

In so doing, President Johnson had some precedent in the Kennedy administration. John Kennedy had personalized the office in terms of style. Every president is likely to place the stamp of his style on the office. Within limits this is inevitable and not necessarily bad. But style can become substantive, or have substantive effects, if not watched. It is likely that personalization has become more common with the growing importance of primaries as the way to nominate. A candidate who gets the nomination through the primaries should think, even though he might not say so publicly, that he has captured the nomination, and that it therefore belongs to him and to his supporters, rather than to the party.

John Kennedy, without a nod to the Democratic party,

had appointed his own choices to the three highest cabinet posts: for secretary of state, Dean Rusk, who had no standing among Democrats or any identification with its established foreign policy positions; for secretary of defense, Robert McNamara, from the automobile industry, with no record in the Democratic party; and for attorney general, Robert Kennedy. The latter appointment was questionable on three counts: Robert Kennedy's role in the campaign, his record in the law profession, and blood relationship. It is likely that if John Kennedy had announced during his campaign his intention to appoint his brother attorney general, he might well have lost the election. Certainly the prospective appointment would have been a campaign issue. The same response would have followed if Nixon had, in the campaign of 1968, announced that once elected, he would appoint his campaign chairman, John Mitchell, as attorney general.

The Johnson nomination as the candidate of the Democratic party in 1964 was certain. So was the party platform. The one uncertainty, or what seemed to be an uncertainty, was the choice of a vice presidential running mate. It became evident early that the President had a problem, not because he needed vice presidential support on the ticket, but because he had to have a running mate. He had two concerns: one was a fear that Bobby Kennedy might make a bid for that office, or that popular demand in the party might force that choice; his second concern was to create some excitement and uncertainty at the convention.

The potential for a Kennedy challenge was, it seems, more real than many politicians thought, as the convention approached. Johnson's concern, then, was not based on paranoia, as some commentators suggested, but on a serious possibility that Robert Kennedy could be moved by some of his supporters and advisers to challenge.

The first major move made by Johnson to eliminate or discourage the Kennedy movement was an announcement in early 1964 that the President was eliminating all cabinet members from vice presidential consideration. This action had significance only as it affected two cabinet members, Bobby Kennedy, the attorney general, and Adlai Stevenson, who had cabinet status as United Nations ambassador. The rumor mills of Washington at the time reported that the President had informed the attorney general earlier that he was not going to pick him as a running mate, and that he hoped Kennedy might take himself out of the running, but that Kennedy had refused to let the public think that the decision had been his, thus forcing the President to act.

The method used, cutting the whole cabinet out of consideration only to eliminate one or two members from consideration, could well have been a direct transfer from Johnson's experience in handling cattle. The regular practice for getting one animal out of a herd is not to try to single the one out for separation, but to take several others with it, then, after corralling the group, those not wanted could be returned to the herd.

The elimination of Robert Kennedy left Johnson with the problem of limited choice. Even before his announcement of the exclusion of cabinet members from consideration, Johnson had, in what seemed a defense against either Kennedy move, named a disproportionate number of Catholic senators as prospective vice presidents. The list at one point included Senator Mansfield of Montana, Senator Muskie of

Maine, Senator Dodd of Connecticut, and me, with Senator Humphrey as the sole non-Catholic. As the convention time neared, for no reason clear to me, the press began to reduce the number of contenders, leaving Humphrey and me as the serious contenders. President Johnson, as time passed, seemed to acknowledge this limitation of his choice.

I was running for reelection to the Senate from Minnesota that year, and attention as a possible vice presidential candidate was not harmful to my campaign, although the prospect of selection, something never taken very seriously by me or by my Minnesota supporters, did complicate the campaign. Some of my supporters for the vice presidency, a few from Minnesota but most from other states, were more seriously interested in the vice presidency than I was.

There was never any direct discussion between the President and me about the office of vice president. But persons very close to the President did give me encouragement, not that I might be chosen, but that I present myself as a possible choice.

Before leaving for the convention in Atlantic City, I had my staff check with the White House staff to make it clear to those with whom we had been speaking that I did not wish to embarrass the President at the convention (or to be embarrassed) and would be glad to drop out. They asked, even urged, me not to do so. I then set up a very modest headquarters in Atlantic City, not at a convention hotel but at a hotel on the edge of town, almost hidden, with the principal purpose of keeping in touch with the White House.

The most positive effort my people made was to bring a campaign picturebook, one prepared for my Senate campaign, and give it limited distribution in convention hotels. The press described the book as elaborately prepared to advance my vice presidential candidacy. It was nothing such. The foreword carried a letter from Lyndon Johnson recommending my reelection to the Senate. This was another example of a characteristic of the press I had long observed and had advised them of, namely, that many members of the press were like my son, who, when he was four years old, had carefully managed to fill a whole page of lined paper with scrawls, never crossing a line. When he asked me to read his work, I suggested that he read it, since he had written it, to which he replied, "Daddy, I can write but I cannot read."

The book in question had long been prepared for my Senate campaign and had been distributed in barber shops, beauty shops, and various other places in Minnesota before being brought to Atlantic City.

Other than the distribution of the book, I participated in two activities that might have been called campaigning for the office. One was a "Meet the Press" program, on the Sunday before the convention, in which I had laid out my conception of the constitutional and traditional view of the vice presidency. At that time I had few significant policy differences with the President. He had pushed ahead on civil rights in 1964 as he finished the Kennedy administration, and he promised to do more. He was running against what was described not just as a militaristic Goldwater approach to international relations, but a "belligerent one." There was no reason to believe that Johnson would alter economic policies that were working well. He was committed to the fulfillment of the promise of the New Deal and was asserting that he would not send American boys to do what Asian boys should do for themselves, a statement interpreted to mean that he would not escalate the war or the American involvement in Vietnam.

Senator Humphrey appeared on a similar "Meet the Press" interview on the same Sunday. Johnson reportedly watched the programs and announced himself pleased with both performances.

The second campaign activity was a press conference in Atlantic City, which I held in response to a demand by the press, who were desperate for news and for something to do. The conference did not come to very much. I remember only one question, which was: "Where will you campaign if chosen?" I answered, remembering a couplet from an old railroad song titled "Tank Town," in which the refrain was, "Tank Town, Tank Town, where the woodbine climbs and the thistles blow," and said quite likely, "where the DC Threes and the Convairs fly."

The afternoon of the day before the President was to announce his choice of vice president, the Washington newspapers carried reports of a casual press conference given by the President. In the course of the conference, the President pointed out that the polls showed that he needed no help from a vice presidential candidate and that he would, in fact, be hurt some by any one of the candidates being named. He went on to list the qualifications he was looking for in his running mate. Upon reading them, I said that no one would quite meet his requirements, except himself.

Even before reading the press reports, it was my opinion that, barring unforeseen developments, Senator Humphrey was the likely choice, and that our request for some information on how the choice was to be announced was not going to be granted.

President Johnson had told the Humphrey people to line up public support. He had not urged me to do so, nor had we attempted to do so. A group of governors endorsed the Humphrey candidacy. Walter Reuther did so, saying that I, not having been on the Foreign Relations Committee of the Senate, was not ready to deal with foreign policy—a new standard for selection. Other farm, liberal, and labor groups endorsed Humphrey. This was somewhat understandable under the circumstances, not as a measure of Humphrey's strength against mine, but as a kind of act of obeisance to Johnson—a demonstration of submission to his branding iron.

I could understand the action of the governors and some of the other groups, but when Humphrey supporters did the same thing in the Minnesota delegation to the convention, I looked upon the action as one of abject surrender to Johnson's demands or, if he had not demanded it, an action similar to that of knights trying to anticipate the king's desires and wishing to please him.

Still with no word from the White House, I decided, with counsel from some others, to remove myself from consideration. That evening I prepared for transmission to the President the next morning:

DEAR MR. PRESIDENT: THE TIME FOR YOUR ANNOUNCEMENT OF YOUR CHOICE OF YOUR VICE PRESIDENTIAL RUNNING MATE IS VERY CLOSE. I HAVE, AS YOU KNOW, DURING THIS CONVENTION AND FOR SEVERAL WEEKS, NOT BEEN INDIFFERENT TO THE CHOICE

YOU MUST MAKE. THE ACTION THAT I HAVE TAKEN HAS BEEN TO
THIS END AND TO THIS PURPOSE: THAT YOUR CHOICE WOULD BE
A FREE ONE AND THAT THOSE WHOM YOU MIGHT CONSULT OR
WHOM MIGHT MAKE RECOMMENDATIONS TO YOU, MIGHT BE WELL
INFORMED. THE GREAT MAJORITY OF THE DELEGATES HERE ARE,
AS YOU KNOW, READY TO SUPPORT YOUR CHOICE. IT IS MY
OPINION THAT THE QUALIFICATIONS THAT YOU HAVE LISTED OR
WHICH YOU ARE SAID TO HAVE LISTED AS MOST DESIRABLE IN THE
MAN WHO WOULD BE VICE PRESIDENT WITH YOU, WOULD BE MET
MOST ADMIRABLY BY SENATOR HUMPHREY. I WISH, THEREFORE,
TO RECOMMEND FOR YOUR PRIMARY CONSIDERATION, SENATOR
HUBERT HUMPHREY.

The next morning I instructed a staff person to send the
wire, release it to the press, then call the White House and
report what had been done. I appointed another staff person
to see that the first one had followed instructions. There are
critical times when the Communist policy of sending a comrade to watch another comrade is advisable.

The White House spokesman, on receiving our call, still
urged us not to send the wire, or release it. Both things had
been done. I was relieved by the release, as were many of my
friends and supporters, some of whom seemed to think that
I was in great political jeopardy. They had had visions of me
dancing while "the Texan shot at my feet" or of my sitting
like a spinster on the front porch while Lyndon went off
with another girl.

I was not as concerned about the possibility of humiliation as were some of my friends. Possibly because I had
never considered Johnson as threatening as he was reputed
to be. I had spent much time with Texas members of the
House of Representatives during my ten years there, often

eating at the Texas table, sometimes with Rayburn in attendance. There was among them a kind of reverence for Sam Rayburn, whom they referred to as "The Man." Lyndon was customarily referred to when he was majority leader in the Senate as "The Other Man." The tone was not quite mocking, but it was far from reverent.

I did not see myself as dancing while Johnson shot at my feet, for I remembered a story my father told of an experience of his while buying cattle in Texas. He had bought, he reported, two carloads of cattle from a Texas rancher. The cattle had to be driven to the railroad loading yards and delivered two weeks later. My father was there to receive the cattle, settle for them, and ship them. On his arrival, he went with the rancher to look at the cattle in the stockyard pens. They were not, my father said to the rancher, the cattle he had bought, but of inferior quality. My father knew it was showdown time. He was tall, just under six feet three inches, weighing about 175 pounds. He never affected any of the dress of the cattle dealers or buyers. His usual dress, almost a uniform, was a gray suit, a gray hat, a white shirt and a tie, with dress shoes protected around cattle yards by rubbers. He often wore gloves. His only concession to the customs of the trade was to carry a rough cattle-prodding cane when in the pen or yard, not for effect but for protection. He never wore the Western-style hat some of his colleagues did, or a shirt with a string tie, or cowboy boots.

According to my father's story, the Texan turned, and they looked each other in the eyes. Evidently there was no flinching. The Texan said, "How much will you give me for these?" His hand had been called, and my father bought the cattle.

This story sustained other advice my father gave me.

Somewhere along the way, he had come to own a diamond ring. Every ten years or so he would have the setting changed to bring it up to date. It had some great symbolic value to him. One day, as he was cleaning the ring, he called to my attention the white line around his finger, contrasting with the brown of the rest of his hand. "I never," he said, "take this ring off on cattle trains, around stockyards, in rough hotels, even when asleep or seeming to be asleep." To take the ring off, he said, would let anyone who might have designs on robbery know from the white streak that he did have a ring. If you left it on, he said, such a person would not be sure as to whether you were asleep or not, "but he would know that you were not afraid."

On the afternoon of the day I sent the withdrawal wire, the President called me to say that he had made his decision to select Senator Humphrey. He made a point in the conversation to say that he had made the decision before he had received my telegram. I was tempted to say, "Six months before you got it," but didn't, saying something like, "That's fine."

I never did learn what the scenario would have been if I had not sent the wire. Quite possibly, I would have been asked to play it out in the way Senator Dodd was when asked to come to the White House along with Senator Humphrey prior to the formal announcement of the Humphrey choice. Dodd told me about the trip and the meeting with the President. He was called, the senator said, by the President and asked to be at the Atlantic City airport at an appointed time. There, he was told, he would meet someone he knew. He went, and met Senator Humphrey. Neither was quite sure why the other was there. On arrival at the White

House, Senator Dodd was taken in first to see the President and Senator Humphrey was left waiting in the anteroom. Then, said Dodd, there followed the strangest conversation of his political career, running something like this. The President said, "Tom, it's good to see you." Dodd replied, "It's good to see you." The President said, "Tom, you're one of my oldest friends." Dodd said, "Mr. President, you're one of my oldest friends." The President said, "How is Grace (Dodd's wife)?" Senator Dodd replied, "She's fine. How is Lady Bird?" The President replied that she was fine, and so it went, for twenty minutes, with no reference to the vice presidential nomination. It ended with the President saying, "It's good to have seen you, Tom." Senator Dodd responded with the same thought and was then escorted from the room.

Senator Humphrey was then, by newspaper account, taken into the room and given the final and certain information that he had been chosen. Although the President had sent Jim Rowe, as a messenger, to Humphrey the night before to tell him of what was to come, Humphrey still seemed uncertain. The extent to which Lyndon was directing, or attempting to direct, the convention, and the acceptance of that direction by some may have been shown in Mrs. Humphrey's comment to my wife regarding my wire: "You mean the President didn't know Gene was going to send that wire?"

The White House called me later the same day to ask me to nominate Humphrey. With some reluctance I accepted. I objected principally to the ritualistic nature of the process, although I had no political or personal objection to speaking for Hubert. I had nominated him for the presidency at the

1952 Democratic convention, had openly supported him for the vice presidency at the 1956 convention, and had campaigned for him in the Wisconsin and West Virginia primaries in 1960.

I gave, I thought, a good speech, although it received little attention at the convention or in the press. In the speech I said a few things about Barry Goldwater as a prophet of despair and as the greatest "no sayer" in recent history. I pictured him standing outside the conference room of decisions, shouting objections from the corridor of "no commitment." Shortly before the convention, the senator had kept a Senate committee from acting for lack of a majority by standing outside the meeting room. Finally, in a flourish, I described the Republicans as living "in a world of their own; a world in which the calendar has no years, in which the clock has no hands, and in which glasses have no lenses (Senator Goldwater, in a campaign photograph, had put his fingers through the frames of his glasses to show that there was no glass, the bows evidently being worn for some cosmetic purpose)." I described them as living "in that strange world in which the pale horse of death and destruction and the white horse of conquest and victory are indistinguishable." Humphrey was chosen by the convention.

David Brinkley noted the speech and made reference to it in one of his reports. *Life* magazine carried one quotation as noteworthy. But that was about the extent of the press coverage, which is probably as much as a speech nominating a vice president chosen by a president-incumbent should get —especially when the President had previously taken the gavel from the presiding officer of the convention and given Humphrey's name to the convention. Subsequently, while

I was actually giving the speech, Lyndon moved about the hall, shaking hands and slapping people's backs in greeting.

The vice presidential politics of the Republicans in 1964 was a puzzle to most political observers of that year, and remains so. Why did Barry Goldwater pick Congressman William E. Miller as his running mate? I knew Miller in the House of Representatives as a good person, lively and apparently not too serious about his conservativism. He did not seem "destined" to be a political force. In the preliminaries to the Republican convention he did not figure strongly. But he was nominated, it seemed, almost as a whim on the part of the nominee of the convention. Not long after the campaign began, the cry of "Who the hell is William Miller?" was raised. Miller told me that the first time he heard of it was when he went, being Catholic, to my alma mater, St. John's, in Minnesota, to campaign and was met at the student's entrance by a great banner carrying the inscription, "Who the hell is William Miller?"

He ran through the campaign in good spirits. Now dead, he is remembered as the first defeated politician to be picked up for the American Express advertisement, "Nobody knows my name, that's why I carry the American Express card." That ad was somewhat in the same spirit in which Miller had campaigned. It was an action which subsequently could be taken as a sign that one had certainly ended his political career (as when retired Sam Ervin appeared in a similar ad). Previously, the signs of surrender were a little more partisan and subtle. For liberals, a career's end was indicated by the endorsement of the Encyclopedia under the auspices of William Benton, or by going to work for that publication or its producer, Mr. Benton. The sign of retirement for conservatives was their being taken on as editors of some kind by *Reader's Digest*, under the protective wing of Lew Wallace.

The Johnson personalization of the presidency began to show soon after his overwhelming victory in November of 1964. It began to show in the President's language. He began to use the possessive pronoun "my" in relation to more and more things and people. He made reference to "my cabinet," "my party," and "my vice president," and so on, when tradition and institution, to say nothing of personal respect in some cases, would have been better served by the simple "the" or a collective "our."

It was reported that one day when the President was visiting an air force base, he directed an airman to move a helicopter. When the airman said, "I can't move it until my commanding officer tells me to do so," the President said, "Move it. It's my helicopter." This was evidently an extension, as he saw it, of his authority as commander in chief of the armed forces.

Johnson's possessiveness and personalization was demonstrated not just in his language but in his dealings with government institutions and people. As a rule, he appointed qualified persons to the respective offices. But once appointed, he failed to note that the person had taken on a new function and status because of the office he now held. For example, he appointed Abe Fortas to the Supreme Court. Fortas was an able lawyer, well qualified to be on the Supreme Court. But after having appointed him to that post, President Johnson seemed to think that he could use Abe more or less as his private lawyer. In similar fashion, he would ask Arthur Goldberg, ambassador to the United Nations, to take on responsibility for settling a strike which had nothing whatsoever to do with the United Nations. President Johnson confused the roles of the House of Representatives and the Senate when it was convenient for him to do so. Thus, when the House was more supportive of his Vietnam War, he treated the House as if it were equal, if not superior, to the Senate in the area of foreign policy. On the other hand, he treated the Senate as though it were a kind of House of Representatives, a change which he had begun as majority leader of the Senate.

The early and substantive achievements of the Johnson presidency were the passage of the 1964 Civil Rights Act, followed by the 1965 act, the tax bill initiated by President Kennedy, the Medicare bill, Medicaid, and a body of legislation which Lyndon chose to call the basis for the "Great Society." According to friends, he hoped to have his place in history—to make a Rooseveltian mark. He saw the Great Society program as a continuation or completion of the New Deal. It was, in fact, neither. While the New Deal had dealt primarily with the function and structure of government, the Great Society program looked to particulars as functional failure loomed over the horizon. The New Deal stressed economic activity, industrially and agriculturally. It emphasized employment, including the distribution of work through the forty hour week law and through early retirement. Also important was a fair return for work—first in the minimum wage law and then through labor management negotiations, price supports for agriculture, and a decent retirement program. The Medicare bill was consistent with the New Deal concept.

The Great Society program featured federal aid to education (a function which, in New Deal days, was left primarily to state and local governments); federal scholarships at the college level; antipoverty programs; a new emphasis on housing and urban development; additional bills to fight cancer, heart disease, strokes, air and water pollution, roadside billboards, and for the beautification of auto junkyards; and special aid to states participating in the Medicaid programs for the poor.

Additional programs spun off from the core of the Great Society—Head Start was introduced for the preschool student, the Job Corps for those who dropped out, the Neighborhood Youth Corps, and VISTA, a domestic peace corps. Members of Congress put their minds to thinking up new programs. The beginning of a civil service, state and federal, to handle the problems of the "poor people" became evident. Almost everything except potholes and garbage collection had become a federal responsibility.

There were at least three things wrong with the comprehensive programs. One was that they were hastily put together, often without a clear conception of what they were about and where they were headed, as in the case of Head Start. They were also underfunded, and battles began among the offices and agencies conducting the Great Society programs. Outside critics were quick to point out the failures that were inevitable, given the subjects of the Great Society program and its limited resources. Finally, the program led to distraction from what should have been the main concern of reformers, that is, the functional disorders and the shortcomings of the New Deal; emphasis on continuing to deal with the failures and the consequences and symptoms of failure began to dominate politics.

At the same time that these difficulties were beginning to show in Johnson's domestic program, the war in Vietnam was being escalated. Military costs were rising. President Johnson procrastinated, believing that the war would be short and inexpensive. Jawboning was tried. The President called in one hundred business leaders and persuaded them to reduce their expansion budgets by ten percent. Interest rates went up. Wages, prices, and capital investments increased; inflation began. The war continued to escalate.

Significant expansion of the United States military presence in Vietnam took place in 1965. President Kennedy had increased the number of military personnel in Vietnam from the approximately 900 put there by Eisenhower to about 17,000. This increase, although described as purely quantitative, was in fact more than that. The increase in numbers was said to be necessary to provide protection to our military advisers. They inevitably did more. The simple quantitative increase from 900 to 17,000 persons, even though the role of the additional military units had been no different from that of the first, took on a special character simply because of its number. Nine hundred persons can be moved out of a country rather quickly in four or five aircraft. Seventeen thousand cannot be removed under stress unless through an operation that is bound to look like an evacuation.

The war in Vietnam had been an "offstage" operation until 1965. Throughout most of the year, reports from the State Department and the Defense Department were optimistic, although toward the end of that year there was a lessening of certainty and enthusiasm among the supporters of the war. When I joined the Foreign Relations Committee of the Senate, at the beginning of 1965, the administration sustained, at least publicly, an earlier statement of Robert McNamara and General Maxwell Taylor that "the major part of the United States military task [in Vietnam] can be completed by the end of that year, although there may be a continuing requirement for a limited number of U.S. training personnel."

By the end of 1965, McNamara had become more cautious, although still optimistic. On November 30, 1965, on his return from a trip to Vietnam, the secretary of defense said, "The most vital impression that I'm bringing back is that we have stopped losing the war."

These were scarcely reassuring words on our military status in Vietnam and when coupled with the evidence that the State Department seemed as uncertain about the political situation as McNamara had been about the military were even more disturbing. In February of 1965, Secretary of State Dean Rusk, speaking to twenty-five to thirty senators in a White House meeting, assured them that the government in power in Vietnam, at the time headed by General Nguyen Khanh, was strongly supported and stable, with every indication that it would be effective for a long time. Within a day or two following the secretary's reassuring statement, the Khanh government had been overthrown.

1965 was a warning year. 1966 was the year of hard judgment on the war in Vietnam. In late 1965, Senator Mansfield, accompanied by Senators Aiken, Muskie, Boggs, and Inouye visited Europe and Asia, including Vietnam. Upon their return to the United States, the senators reported their findings and conclusions to the President and, on January 8, 1966, to the Foreign Relations Committee of the Senate. The report was titled, "The Vietnam Conflict: The Substance and the Shadow."

The report proved to be not only accurate in its noting of facts, but prophetic as well. It pointed out that the question "is not one of applying increased U.S. pressure to a defined military situation but rather of pressing on in a military situation which is, in effect, open-ended. . . . "

"All of mainland Southeast Asia, at least," it said, "cannot be ruled out as a potential battlefield." It noted the instability of the South Vietnamese government, observing that the government was "at the beginning of dealing with the problems of popular mobilization in support of the government. They are starting, moreover, from a point considerably behind that which prevailed at the time of Diem's assassination." The report warned that the enormous increase in military participation by the United States already begun by the administration might tend to drain the war of any purpose relevant to the Vietnamese people. It cautioned against any false hope of assistance for our efforts from other nations and, in fact, warned that relations with our allies both in Europe and the Far East would become increasingly strained if the scope of the war was expanded. (The only significant commitment of troops, numerically, was from Korea. The commitment was largely symbolic rather than military, and at one point all but came apart because the Korean troops were not being supplied with a favorite food, Kimchi, a kind of fermented cabbage.)

The administration seemed undeterred by the Mansfield report. President Johnson sent the Congress on January 19, 1966, a request for over $13 billion to meet the additional costs of the war in Vietnam. On January 24, when the budget for fiscal year 1967 was submitted, it included requests for $9.1 billion of new allocations for Vietnam expenditures.

It was understood that the administration intended to resume the bombing of North Vietnam following a holiday truce, which had been in effect at the time of the filing of the Mansfield report.

Administration spokesmen, principally the Secretary of State Dean Rusk, appearing before the Senate Foreign Relations Committee, and in other public statements, seemed undisturbed by the criticism of Vietnam policy and by the growing breach between the executive branch of the government and the Senate.

In January, fifteen senators wrote to the President, endorsing the Mansfield report and urging the President not to renew the bombing. The letter did not reflect the full measure of antibombing and anti-Vietnam sentiment in the Senate. Only Democrats were asked to sign, as the authors saw the statement and the war as primarily a responsibility of the Democrats. A number of Senate Republicans and Democrats who did not sign the letter had made public statements against the bombing. John Sherman Cooper, a Republican senator from Kentucky, stated the case of both the signers and that of some of those who had not signed the letter, when he said on January 26, 1966, " . . . bombing should not be resumed now. If bombings are resumed, we will lose, at least for the present, the chance to negotiate, however slim it is."

The President did not respond to the letter directly. His response was a statement referring to the Tonkin Gulf Resolution and a copy of a recent letter he had sent to members of the House of Representatives. Members of the Senate who opposed the war were offended by the President's response on two counts: one, his use of the Tonkin Gulf Resolution in an attempt to stop serious questioning of presidential policies, and two, the use of the letter to the House of Representatives as an answer to the Senate challenge, since this reflected upon the constitutional responsibility for foreign policy, which is quite specifically vested in the Senate. A copy of the letter to the senators sent to the House of Representatives would have been consistent with the constitutional functions of the two bodies. Johnson's action could only be interpreted as a slap at the Senate and as a reflection of his judgment that Senate views on the war were, as far as he was concerned, possibly even less important than those of House members.

The signers of the letter met during the days following the release of the President's response, but came to no agreement on a course of action. Meanwhile, there was evidence that the letter had disturbed the administration, which was moved to defend its position and to attempt to silence criticism. Averell Harriman's services were enlisted.

At the request of the President, senators were invited to the former ambassador's home and, over cocktails, warned of the Communist threat. McGeorge Bundy, the President's assistant for National Security Affairs, and General Maxwell Taylor, who had been ambassador to South Vietnam, made personal visits to the Senate to explain the administration's position. Other messages and messengers were sent. Secretary Rusk appeared before the Foreign Relations Committee at public hearings on January 28. A week later, Secretary of Defense McNamara declined to do so on grounds of national security. His refusal was supported by the President.

The Senate Foreign Relations Committee hearings went on. General Taylor appeared to support administration policy. Retired General James Gavin and former ambassador George Kennan appeared before the committee. Both spoke strongly against the administration's policy of escalating the war.

To distract public attention from the committee hearings, the President flew to a meeting with the South Vietnamese leaders in Honolulu. At the conclusion of the conference, "The Pledge of Honolulu" was issued. The statement, or "pledge," as it was called, went far beyond any declaration of policy for South Vietnam that the administration had made in the past, or anything that Congress had in any formal way been committed to carry out. It included common defense against aggression, work of social revolution, a goal of free self-government, and an attack on hunger, ignorance, and disease—a kind of Great Society program for Southeast Asia.

President Johnson proceeded to escalate the war. On March 9, 1966, American planes carried out the heaviest bombardment of the war. Secretary General U. Thant of the United Nations called for the cessation of the bombing. Demonstrations against the military government in Saigon took place in several large cities in South Vietnam. By April 1966, B-52s from Guam were bombing North Vietnam. The Defense Department acknowledged that civilian protest in South Vietnam was hampering military operations.

Near the end of April, the State Department stated that it was our policy to follow the doctrine of hot pursuit of enemy aircraft into China, if necessary. All of this was almost a point-by-point demonstration of what the Mansfield report had foretold.

Early in 1966, Secretary McNamara estimated that, with the bombing of the North, the capacity to infiltrate would be limited to "up to" 4,500 military personnel a month. By April, the infiltration was estimated at between 5,500 and 7,000 a month, and a further increase in U.S. combat strength was being projected.

When asked in May of 1966 about his early projection of infiltration, McNamara said that "up to" did not mean a ceiling, and that the number the North Vietnamese could infiltrate is "less than X, 'X' being quite a bit in excess of 4,500; but, in any event, there is some ceiling that would result from the bombing of the lines of communications." He never did say what "X" was.

In my mind, and certainly in the minds of other senators who heard the secretary's testimony, his explanation of what the words meant to him contrasted with what they meant to us and added to the growing doubt as to whether one could rely upon him as an observer of the war, as a witness to its progress, or as one who could be trusted to play a major part in the direction of the war.

Distrust in the secretary was not alleviated by other testimony in which he would include facts that were either irrelevant or far afield from the point being raised. For example, in testimony before the Foreign Relations Committee on April 20, 1966, when asked by Senator Morse about our military equipment in Latin America, McNamara replied that "the total number of combat aircraft in Latin America was 547, which is fewer than the combat aircraft in North Korea." He never explained the relationship, if any, between the number of combat aircraft in North Korea and the number in Latin America, or how he was certain that the number was 547, not 500 approximately or about 600. In the same testimony, in response to a similar question, he said that the total number of tanks in Latin America was 974, not 975 or approximately 1,000. He gave the figure without consultation with aides, without reference notes, and then added, "That is sixty percent as many as a single country . . . Bulgaria . . . has."

Although I had resolved earlier that I would never again ask him a question, the reference to Bulgaria moved me to try once more. I asked him for an explanation as to whether there was any relationship between the number of tanks in Latin America and the number in Bulgaria. "Is there a kind of Bulgarian absolute?" I asked. He replied, "If there were, I would be happy to give it to you. I don't know what it is here." I asked him no more questions.

Oil installations in the areas of Hanoi and Haiphong were bombed by the end of June, and in July the South Vietnamese chief of state was saying that the North would be invaded if necessary. Bombing of infantry routes in Laos continued, and at the end of July troop concentrations in and around the demilitarized zone separating the two Vietnams were being bombed by B-52s.

In the fall President Johnson, after the conference in Manila, paid a surprise visit to Vietnam, where he exhorted the troops to "bring home the coonskin." At the same time, Secretary McNamara said that the number of U.S. troops would be increased in 1967. Progress in the war was now being measured and reported in terms of "kill ratios," how many enemy corpses were being counted.

As the end of 1966 approached, the reports were that U.S. advisers were taking an active part in operations in Thailand and that American troops were being moved into the Mekong Delta area, where operations had previously been conducted by the South Vietnamese army. Hanoi was bombed in December, with reports that residential areas were hit, incidentally, in the attempts to destroy military targets.

The process from 1965 to 1967 was properly labeled in Orwellian, Latinized language as "an escalation, not of military force, but of ideological and rationalized support." As the military presence and force increased, the explanation and justification of U.S. participation rose to the level, extent, and intensity required. The war quickly changed from one in which our concern was to settle a civil difference in the South of Vietnam, to stopping an invasion from the North, and then, with an ominous introduction by Secretary Rusk of the threat of a billion Chinese by the year 2000, to eliminating a menace to the future of the free world. The ideological escalation was, much like the military one, a continuum allowing no point of challenge. No right time for negotiations could be marked. It was either too soon or too late. We had either an advantage and, therefore, could wait for the enemy to offer to negotiate, or we were at a disadvantage, and in no position, so the experts said, to negotiate. President Johnson spoke of his willingness to meet anytime on a neutral ship in a neutral sea. Neither the time, the ship, nor the sea were ever found.

The Vietnam War and its continuation were presented as part of the national presidential heritage. President Johnson said that he was carrying on what three presidents before him had supported—Truman in his support of the French, Eisenhower in sending in advisers, and Kennedy in his commitment of potential combat troops, some 17,000. President Nixon was subsequently to say that he was carrying on the tradition of the four preceding presidents, having placed President Johnson in the line-up.

Political attacks on critics of the war became more intense with the escalation of the war. As it continued to go badly, its advocates became more defensive. The motives of those who spoke out against the war were questioned, as was their patriotism and in the case of Democrats their loyalty to the party. Critics were called "nervous Nellies" and "special pleaders," and, in the language of cattle handlers, as ready to "cut and run." In February of 1966, a White House spokesman, using language of the fifties, referred to members of the National Council of Churches who opposed the war as "alleged churchmen." Religion was questioned.

President Johnson, at a Medal of Honor ceremony in December 1966, posed a question about dissenters: Just how patriotic were they?

"The war," he said, "is a cause which deserves not only the bravery of our soldiers, but the patience and fortitude of all our citizens. All of these we have in good supply. It far outweighs the reluctance of men who exercise so well the right of dissent, but let others fight to protect them from those whose very philosophy is to do away with the right to dissent."

In March of that year, a racist theme was injected into the rhetoric when Vice President Hubert Humphrey said, "[Are] the only people you want to die for the whites . . . Are we saying that we're unable to keep our commitments for the brown and yellow people—we can keep them only for whites?"

Prophets of victory spoke in early 1967. In January our ambassador to Vietnam, Henry Cabot Lodge, predicted "sensational" military gains in 1967 and added that open peace negotiations would probably never take place, but rather, that the enemy would merely fade away.

In April the commanding general, William Westmoreland, was brought back and, at the request of the Johnson administration, spoke before the joint meeting of Congress. His message was reassuring. He said that our forces and those of the other free-world allies had grown in strength and profitted from experience. He saw the South Vietnamese army as much improved as "a military force that performs with growing professional skill," as "having scored repeated successes against some of the best Vietcong and North Vietnamese army units." The kill ratio, which in 1965, he said, had been three to one (36,000 of the enemy to 12,000 of the troops of the Republic of Vietnam and its allies—the allies being the United States primarily, for with the exception of Korea, whose assistance we were paying for, other nations were giving little more than humanitarian relief). The general saw the kill ratio as improving, in some weeks reaching as high, he said, as ten or twenty to one in our favor.

The general, then and since, has seemed a man without guile. Several things in his statement were of particular interest. One was his use of the term *kill ratio.* Previously, the Foreign Relations Committee had been told that there was no such measure in use and that it had been dreamed up by the press.

The general moved the war into a new political field in saying that there was, or at least that he had seen, "no evidence that this is an internal insurrection," but "that it is aggression from the North." These remarks were particularly significant in themselves, but also because they were made by a field commander on active duty who had been brought back not only to explain and support a military program, but also to defend the political basis for an expansion of the war.

After Westmoreland's formal presentation to the Congress, President Johnson invited a number of members of Congress to the White House for a more intimate meeting with the general. Martha Raye, who had been visiting troops in Vietnam, was also at the White House. President Johnson asked her to address members of Congress preliminary to the general's remarks. She was wearing a khaki dress, reminiscent of World War I, and told us that our soldiers in Vietnam were brave. The general followed, repeating some of what he had already said, but adding what he labeled as amusing incidents of the war. One incident was the story of an American officer who was proceeding down a Vietnamese road in the company of the South Vietnamese. On observing a group of black pajama–clad persons approaching, the American asked his Vietnamese companions whether the group was friendly or not. He was told that if they passed and smiled, they were friendly. If they threw a hand grenade, that would indicate unfriendliness.

The second light story he told was that of a Vietcong, or North Vietnamese, who had walked the length of the Ho Chi Minh Trail to deliver two mortar shells in South Vietnam. As he arrived at the supply station, he asked the person in charge what he should do with the two shells and was told to place them in the adjacent pile of shells. Then the man again asked the supply officer what he should do. He was told "to go back and get two more."

In June of 1967, our troop strength in Vietnam reached 463,000, and in August an increase to 525,000 was authorized. The "threat from the North" theme was underscored by Secretary McNamara in September of that year, when he announced that the United States would begin deployment of a "China-oriented" (a happy combination of words) antiballistic missile system. Vice President Humphrey spoke forcefully of a Chinese threat. On October 15, 1967, he said that American security was at stake in Asia and that "the threat to world peace is militant, aggressive, Asian Communism, with its headquarters in Peking, China."

The Humphrey speech followed the press conference by Secretary of State Dean Rusk on October 12 in which he spoke of the billion Chinese, armed with nuclear weapons, whom he saw as a danger to Asia and as threatening "doctrinaire and ideological adventurism abroad."

I read in Rusk's remarks a possible move to enlarge the Vietnam War into a war against China, or at least to inject new political and moral considerations into the controversy over the war.

These observations by Rusk were interesting, and in fact are interesting, when set against what he had said about the Chinese in 1951. In that year, before the China Institute in New York, he spoke of the "greedy hands" of Russia, stretching out to dismember China, and of China as being "sacrificed to the ambitions of the Communist conspiracy." China, he said, had been driven into "an adventure of foreign aggression (namely in Korea)."

Ideological, historical, and personal forces that had been developing over a period of more than twenty years since the end of World War II all bore on the Vietnam War in

1967. Rusk's belief, his insistence, that the United States had to maintain an anti-Communist bastion in South Vietnam as part of the overall strategy of containing Communism was an extension of the strategic theory developed by John Foster Dulles. That is, a kind of modern Cromwellian approach, combining declarations of moral justification sustained by legal covenants to be supported by military action. The military involvement reflected the post–World War II arrogance of the U.S. military. The word was that the French had not fought well, if at all, in World War II, so why should they be expected to fight well in a colonial war in Southeast Asia. Under Eisenhower, it was believed, our military could first advise them and subsequently exhibit our superiority in military action. Air power, it was believed, could take care of the Vietcong and the North Vietnamese. There was talk of bombing them back into the Stone Age. The helicopter— a new version called the attack helicopter—was introduced as a mechanical variation of the cavalry. Added to these two driving forces was the reputation of Robert McNamara, which combined his own personal attributes with the qualities generally considered held by men who were presidents of major automobile companies, that is, that they are unable to make mistakes. McNamara, of Ford Motors, succeeded Charlie Wilson of General Motors, who had been secretary of defense under President Eisenhower. The earmark of the McNamara secretariat was to be quantification of defense systems analyses and contingency planning.

The opposition to the war and to forces supporting it seemed small and weak as 1967 began. Protests against the war were scattered and easily dismissed as involving only fringe groups or unstable persons. The first significant expression of widening and changing judgment of the war occurred at the conference of Clergy and Laymen Concerned about Vietnam. The meeting took place in Washington, D.C., in February 1967. The participants could not be dismissed as "alleged churchmen" or as "peaceniks" or "pacifists." Many came from very conservative churches and synagogues. They came from all over the country and included religious leaders of established reputation, such as Dr. John Bennett of Union Theological Seminary, Rabbi Abraham Heschel of the Jewish Theological Seminary of America, Philip Scharper of the Catholic publishing house Sheed and Ward, Reverend Eugene Carson Blake of the World Council of Churches, Father Joseph Mulligan of the Jesuit university Fordham, Robert McAfee Brown, professor of religion at Stanford University, Bishop John Wesley Lord, United Methodist Bishop of the Washington, D.C. area, and others. The conference was the first major call to the nation to question the justification for our involvement in the war. Three members of the U.S. Senate spoke at the meeting: Senator Morse of Oregon, Senator Ernest Gruening of Alaska, and myself.

Following the conference, either because of it or from other motivations, persons, organizations and publications took up the antiwar cause. The Women's International League for Peace and Freedom became actively involved. Publications such as *Christianity in Crisis* and *Commonweal* carried articles and editorials critical of the war. Protests continued on college campuses. Poets took up the cause. Robert Bly wrote a poem called "Counting Small-Boned Bodies," and John Haag composed "Kilroy," noting that Kilroy was not in Vietnam. And so it went, outside politics and outside the Senate, where opposition seemed limited to a small number of senators.

The President had been advised and urged privately to end the war. The Senate Committee on Foreign Relations had made the public case against the war. Yet the President pursued and expanded the war. There was little reason to believe after the Senate voted in 1966 against debate on the war—with only five senators voting in favor of the action— that the war could be challenged in any way other than in the presidential election of 1968. I gave up any hope that the Senate was likely to act with any strength against the war in Vietnam when on March 1, 1966, Senator Morse of Oregon, offered a motion to bring up the Vietnam War for reexamination. Senator Mansfield of Montana, the majority leader of the Senate, proposed to table the Morse amendment. This, I thought, was a surprising move on Mansfield's part, since the move of Senator Morse was clearly within the range of Senate rights and responsibility, and the Mansfield motion was clearly in the service of the Johnson administration. Mansfield's move was an attempt to silence the Senate on the issue, or if not to silence it, to cut off formal procedures; when the vote was taken, only five senators voted against the tabling motion, Senators Fulbright, Gruening, Morse, Young, and I. Among those who voted with Mansfield were both Robert and Ted Kennedy and George McGovern. The vote was 92 to 5.

At the end of November 1967, I announced that I would challenge Lyndon Johnson. Our first plan was to concentrate on four "critical primaries" regionally distributed: Massachusetts in the Northeast, Wisconsin in the Midwest, Oregon in the Northwest, and California—with the possibility of adding New York, a primary different from all others. New Hampshire was added later, under urging from Democrats in New Hampshire and some pressure from restless troops.

Although the public image of that campaign is one of happy students walking through the snow, being greeted at doorsteps by winter-bound natives, it was actually one in which the Johnson administration and Johnson partisans conducted a vigorous, sometimes vicious campaign.

In mid-December, an administration spokesman announced that everyone in the administration would campaign against me and that there would be a massive organizational effort by Democratic state officials directed by the Democratic National Committee. The plan, the story said, had already been put into effect in New Hampshire, Wisconsin, Nebraska, and California. Few administration officials came into New Hampshire, evidently because they thought victory was a sure thing. They did, however, come into Wisconsin, including the vice president, the Secretary of Agriculture Orville Freeman, Attorney General Ramsey Clark, Secretary of Housing and Urban Development Robert Weaver, and others. The Johnson campaign in New Hampshire was largely left to the state Democrats. The Democratic governor, repeating a phrase used by Dean Rusk, said that a significant vote for me "would be greeted by cheers in Hanoi," thus striking a theme that was to be used by those opposed to me. Six months later, at the close of the California primary, Senator Kennedy invoked this theme in our television debate when he charged that I would "negotiate with Communists."

The regular Democrats in New Hampshire ran advertisements stating "The Communists in Vietnam are watching the New Hampshire primary." A second form of attack was used by Senator McIntyre, a Democrat, in a commercial radio broadcast on the Monday before the election, in which he accused me of having proposed laws "to let American draft dodgers . . . return home scot-free without punishment," a gross misinterpretation of what I had proposed. This action on McIntyre's part, which was out of character, moved me to ask him, as I boarded a plane leaving New Hampshire the morning after the election, what he was doing "riding first class."

A singular and unprecedented effort was made by the Democratic party organization in New Hampshire in distributing serial-numbered pledge cards to registered Democrats, which in effect asked them to vote not in private but in public.

Reporters and political experts were so wrong about much of the campaign of 1968 that many, had they professional integrity, would have put away their typewriters and written no more of politics. The "expert" opinion generally held that I would possibly get 12 percent of the New Hampshire vote. Not counting write-ins, which were not included in the official count, I got 42 percent of the vote and a majority of the delegates. With write-ins counted, the difference between President Johnson's vote and mine was 230 votes.

On Sunday, March 31, two days before the Wisconsin primary, President Johnson addressed the nation on television. He spoke of his interest in deescalating the war. American bombing, he said, would be restricted. At the end of that speech, he went beyond the printed text which had been distributed to announce that he would not be a candidate for the Democratic nomination.

I do not know what the immediate motivation for the Johnson withdrawal was. The polls indicated that I would get 60 percent of the vote in the Wisconsin primary. Although Johnson had not campaigned in the state himself, he had made a substantial effort through his staff and cabinet, in contrast with that in New Hampshire. As late as March 29, Vice President Humphrey predicted that the President would be the Democratic nominee in November, and on March 28, Richard Nixon, campaigning in Wisconsin, predicted victory for the President.

The entrance of Robert Kennedy into the campaign beyond Wisconsin may have had some bearing on the President's choice.

The President gave as his principal reason for dropping out, his wish to avoid being accused of political motives for what he might subsequently do in his conduct of the war.

My immediate thought, and hope, was that this indicated that President Johnson intended to end the war or deescalate it. It did not. What his withdrawal did was to put him in a position to influence more effectively the process of picking the Democratic nominee as well as determining the Democratic platform position on the war. It left him free to get on with the war relatively free of personal responsibility.

The President faced a hard choice. He could quite likely have been renominated, had he chosen to fight for the nomination. Possibly he could have been reelected, but he was faced by the likelihood of having to acknowledge that he had lost power and did not control the issues. It was a classical choice between keeping the office or giving it up and thereby avoiding any possibility of failure, at the same time putting himself in a position to strongly influence, if not control, politics and government in order to vindicate his position. His choice, manifest in his withdrawal, was to retain power, limited though it might be over the war. This became preferable to pursuing the office of the presidency, struggling to hold on to it, and losing power in the process.

ROBERT KENNEDY IN 1968

IN MARCH 1967 in speaking with James Wechsler of the *New York Post,* I said that I thought Senator Robert Kennedy would be the strongest candidate to challenge President Johnson and the war if he chose to run.

Senator Kennedy, however, made no move in 1967 that indicated he might take up the challenge. He publicly declared his support for President Johnson and did not join any of the organized Senate actions against administration policy.

At a press breakfast sponsored by the *Christian Science Monitor* on January 30, 1968, Senator Kennedy, when asked about my campaign, said, "I think it is being helpful to President Johnson." When asked whether he would run, he said, "No, I can't conceive of any circumstances in which I would run."

When pressed harder to be clearer in his rejection of a campaign he said, "All right, in no foreseeable circumstances." In a private meeting with me, Kennedy said that he would not run, adding that he had to "think about his future." I thought that he had made a commitment to me not to run.

There was other evidence that he would not run. Close friends and former supporters of John Kennedy, such as

Dick Goodwin and Arthur Schlesinger, Jr., had, in early February, supported me, saying that Kennedy would not run. The evidence was clear to me that he intended to stand by what he had said to me. I believed that he would not come into the foray after I had declared and begun my campaign. This was not to be the case. On March 13, the day after the New Hampshire primary, Senator Robert Kennedy told a reporter that he was "reassessing" his position as to whether he would run against President Johnson. Senator Kennedy, or his office, called my office in Washington several times on the morning after New Hampshire, asking to see me when I returned to Washington. I saw him the afternoon of that day, about 4:30 P.M. in his brother Edward's Senate office. The meeting lasted about fifteen minutes. Not much came of it. Although he did not say what he intended to do, I got the definite impression that he was going to run. I told him that I was going to continue my campaign, suggesting that there were primaries in which I was not entered and that he might consider running in those.

About the time that Senator Kennedy announced his candidacy, the national press reported that he had offered to stay out of the race if President Johnson would name a commission to redirect the nation's Vietnam policy. Senator Kennedy did not mention the commission idea when we met on March 13. There is some disagreement whether the idea of the presidential commission originated with Senator Kennedy, with Theodore Sorensen, with Mayor Richard Daley of Chicago, or with someone else. Senator Kennedy, in a statement of the matter reported in the *New York Times* of March 18, 1968, indicated that he would not have begun his effort to gain the nomination in 1968 if it had been evident that a change in Vietnam policy was forthcoming. The President's rejection of the commission proposal made it clear that no change was to come about. Senator Kennedy was quoted as saying that "so long as Lyndon B. Johnson is President, our Vietnam policy will not change."

It was difficult for me to conceive of Senator Kennedy's having made such an offer with any possible belief that President Johnson or any other president of the United States could consider it, even for a day, as it was reported Johnson did. The President may have been stunned. I doubt he gave the proposition any serious attention.

The day before Senator Kennedy's March 16 announcement, I was told that Senator Ted Kennedy wanted to make an unpublicized trip to Wisconsin that night to meet with me. Arriving in Green Bay after nine o'clock in the evening, I was told that Senator Kennedy and members of his staff, and some of my staff traveling with him, had left Washington too late to make the airline connections in Chicago and were attempting to charter a plane to Green Bay. As late as eleven o'clock the Green Bay airport responded that no flight plan had been filed, and so assuming that the party would arrive the next morning, I went to bed.

I was awakened some time after one o'clock. The manager of the hotel offered the use of the back entrance and freight elevator to bring the senator to my suite.

He arrived, and in no time the suite was crowded with people. In addition to the senator, there were members of my staff, such as Dick Goodwin, who was in transition, members of my family, and the campaign committee. It was like a family gathering for a matchmaking, some of them hoping for an engagement, others not.

Like the walrus and the carpenter, Senator Kennedy and I talked of many things. We talked about the campaign and the way it was developing, of the public opposition to the administration's policy, of his recent trip to South Vietnam to investigate corruption in the civil government, and of the St. Patrick's Day Parade in Boston, in which we were both scheduled to march. Someone suggested that we might want to speak privately in the bedroom suite.

We went into the bedroom, but our conversation there was no different from what it had been in the living room of the suite. Finally, he indicated that his brother would announce his candidacy the following day. I said that the announcement could make no significant change in my announced purposes and objectives. Had anything more happened at the meeting, it would have been well publicized, as there were enough witnesses.

Throughout the meeting, Senator Kennedy kept at his side a black briefcase, new and shiny and, I believe, plastic —quite unlike the kind of briefcase one expects Harvard men to carry. He was about to leave when I observed that one of the clasps on the case was open; I suggested that he might want to close it lest someone outside think that he had opened it while he was in the suite. He laughed and pushed down the clasp. Our people concluded that a tape recorder was enclosed in the bright, shiny case.

The reports of the meeting were generally quite accurate, the only uncertainty being over who had called for the meeting. I decided after reading reports of what Senator Edward Kennedy had to say about it that he believed the initiative was mine. I had been led to believe that the initiative was his. I think we were both right or wrong, and that somehow it was suggested to each of us—possibly by the same persons—that the other wanted the meeting.

The press almost immediately began to talk of my withdrawal, some newspaper persons going so far as to say that I had been a stalking horse all the time, knowingly or unknowingly. Kennedy supporters fed the line. Richard Rovere, still a respected and published political expert, wrote in the *New Yorker* of March 23, 1968, that support for me came not out of any personal attachment to me, but rather out of hostility toward Lyndon Johnson, and that the young people who had been drawn to my campaign were intelligent enough (or at least as intelligent as Rovere, one might conclude) not to let their loyalty to me stand in the way of their switching to Senator Kennedy if it appeared that I could not win.

Some seasoned liberal political figures did defect: Arthur Schlesinger and Dick Goodwin were the most notable, along with some young activists. But most of the students who had been involved in my campaigns, as well as the adults, stayed with me, and many more joined. The enthusiasm of the crowds was greater than it had been before Robert Kennedy's entrance, and within a week both the number of volunteers and unsolicited contributions also increased greatly.

Once Senator Kennedy entered the campaign, I felt that neither he nor I could be nominated.

Although as the campaign went on through Indiana, Nebraska, and Oregon, Kennedy publicly talked of a willingness to work out an accord and expressed hope that we would be able to work together, he did not at any time say that he would support me if I were nominated.

Our first effort at accommodation was over the District of Columbia delegation. I thought that we had agreed to let it go uncontested and accept whatever delegation was chosen, without a Kennedy-McCarthy factional fight. Kennedy spokesmen quickly announced that we had yielded the delegation to Kennedy.

After the Nebraska vote, Pierre Salinger, as a press spokesman, issued a public statement saying that I was not a "credible" candidate. I assume he meant to say "creditable."

But it was in Indiana that we got the first reading on the kind of campaign the Kennedy camp planned to run—a campaign similar to that which Robert Kennedy had run against Republican Senator Robert Keating for the New York Senate seat, which Kennedy had won. That campaign was properly appealed to the Fair Campaign Practices Committee. The tactics were of the kind that members of Congress characterize as cheap and petty.

The distortion and misrepresentation of my voting record was circulated by an organization called Citizens for Kennedy. The "fact sheet," as it was called, appeared in various forms: as a letter addressed to my Massachusetts supporters, then presented on university campuses as paid advertisements. Local Democratic organizations received some forms of the sheet. It was given national distribution by what were called volunteer organizations in Indiana, Nebraska, South Dakota, and California. Senator Kennedy publicly denied the pamphlet and the advertisements in May, but in the California debate a few weeks later, when asked about the attacks, said that he did not know to what I was referring. Sometime after the California primary, I asked one of the Kennedy people just who had been responsible for the voting record operation and was told that it was Pierre Salinger. The *New York Times* took on the distortion, but the best response to it was a letter to the editor of *The Daily Bruin*, a student newspaper at the University of California:

> It is alarming to see the lengths to which Kennedy supporters are going already, not so much to illuminate what their candidate stands for, as to discredit Senator McCarthy. The ad which appeared in *The Daily Bruin* on Wednesday has come out in a number of college newspapers and seems to have taken a great deal of time and effort to get at the "facts." Unfortunately, the authors of this ad have resorted to some fantastic misrepresentations, either by taking some issues out of the context of the bills in which they were presented by not mentioning that McCarthy voted for stronger, more enforcible legislation than some of the vaguely worded passages that they cite. . . .
>
> It may seem strange to Mike Shatzkin, who wrote an article to go with the paid advertisement, that many of us who have been attracted to McCarthy have doubts about a lot of things, including the demand by Shatzkin that we must support Bobby unquestioningly, without doubts.
>
> The pretense of both the ad and Shatzkin that they are somehow presenting the "truth" is especially insulting being presented within an academic community, but its cynicism has somewhat the same ring as that displayed by the senator from New York, when he announced that he was going to win the presidency of

the United States, while supporting Senator McCarthy.
. . . Many of us have been extremely concerned about the "credibility gap" which has grown between the government and the people. I suggest that from the way Kennedy has been running the campaign and from the way his own record looks, both before and after he decided that he was to be president, that if he is elected, we will be faced with a credibility gap that will make that of the present administration look like a crack in the plaster.

The experience of these attacks, misrepresentations, and distortions was the most disappointing part of the entire campaign. Their effect was not measurable, but nearly a year after they were first published—after the campaign was over —when I was scheduled to speak at the University of Notre Dame, I was given a copy of the school newspaper in which a student went on at great length still using the same misrepresentations. Similar misrepresentations of my record on civil rights were made to the black press. We tried to counter the falsehoods with a report of my record, as approved by civil rights organizations over a period of twenty years in Congress. Insofar as we could discover, only one black newspaper challenged the Kennedy campaign misstatements.

This dishonest attack was most surprising, since, Kennedy in a forum for newspapermen sponsored by the *Christian Science Monitor,* on January 30, 1968, the same conference at which he announced that he would not run, said that healing the race question was what the campaign should be about, and said that to do so one must appeal to the generous spirit of Americans. "McCarthy," he added, "is unable to tap this spirit."

How he thought reconciliation would be advanced by an attempt to turn blacks against me, he never explained. Nor did he explain how the good will of whites was to be gained by his statement to the white population of Orange County, California, that I would move ten thousand blacks into Orange County—a complete fabrication on his part.

The entrance of Robert Kennedy into the campaign immediately divided the antiwar forces and introduced the element of power politics. The divisive effect might have been limited had the President stayed in the race, or the vice president entered the primaries. But with neither Johnson nor Humphrey in the primaries except in a peripheral, vicarious way, the campaigns in most states were reduced to contests between the two antiwar candidates.

Kennedy's campaign also introduced a direct attack on President Johnson. I had not in my campaign attacked the President's integrity, character, or motives. Following his withdrawal, the President invited Senator Kennedy and me, separately, to the White House. My discussion with him was almost pro forma and casual. The only departure occurred when Senator Kennedy's name came up. The President said nothing, but drew the side of his hand across his throat.

Soon after the announcement of his candidacy, Senator Kennedy, in a speech given in Los Angeles on March 24, charged the President with "calling upon the darker impulses in the American spirit, not perhaps deliberately, but through his action and the example he sets—an example where integrity, truth, honor, and all the rest feel like words to fill out speeches rather than as guiding beliefs."

Senator Kennedy was reported as having said that he would drop out if he lost Oregon. He lost that primary but did not drop out and went on to California. The culmination of that campaign was the joint appearance of the senator and me on ABC's "Issues and Answers" on the Sunday before the Tuesday California primary. Almost from the day of his entering the campaign in March, I had been asking for debate. He had consistently refused. But because, we thought, he feared a loss in California, he accepted the ABC offer; not the debate format we had proposed, one modeled on the Kennedy-Nixon debate of 1960, but rather a kind of joint press conference. The debate was not much more than a press conference, except for three statements made by Kennedy. First, he said that I would negotiate with Communists. The implication was that he would not. Just how the war in Vietnam would be ended without negotiating with Communists he never explained, nor did he explain negotiations during his brother's administration with Communists in Russia, in China, and especially in Cuba.

His second statement had it that I would move ten thousand blacks from Watts into Orange County; the third that he would give jets to Israel, something the Israelis were not then asking for and certainly no matter of controversy between him and me. He had, I discovered later, made a similar statement before Jewish audiences in California. Senator Kennedy won the California primary by 140,000 votes. He received 1,445,880 votes; I received 1,305,728.

Following the debate, I concluded that I could not support Robert Kennedy for the presidency, a judgment based on consideration of his campaign tactics, questions about whether he could be trusted with the power of the presidency, and as a final consideration, his charges and assertions in the debate. Even his antiwar position was becoming clouded. Vice President Humphrey remarked in the campaign that "Robert Kennedy and I came to hold remarkably similar positions on the war."

On the night of the election, after he had finished making a victory statement, Robert Kennedy was assassinated. The act seemed so out of context, so random, like something from a Camus novel, as to deny rational explanation. I think the best statement of Senator Kennedy's character, and of his campaign, was written by the poet Robert Lowell, a friend of Robert Kennedy, and of mine:

R.F.K.
For Robert Kennedy 1925–68

Here in my workroom, in its listlessness
of Vacancy, like the old townhouse we shut for summer,
airtight and sheeted for old summers,
far from the hornet yatter of his gang—
its loneliness, a thin smoke thread of vital
air. But what will anyone teach you now?
Doom was woven in your nerves, your shirt,
woven in the great clan; they too were loyal,
and you too more than loyal to them, to death.
For them like a prince, you daily left your tower
to walk through dirt in your best cloth. Untouched,
alone in my Plutarchan bubble, I miss
you, you out of Plutarch, made by hand—
forever approaching our maturity.

After the assassination of Robert Kennedy, the chance of carrying the antiwar issue at the Democratic convention was, barring unforeseen developments, lost. The party was committed to defending the war policies of the Johnson administration. Senator Muskie, who had established his claim to the vice presidency by presenting the Johnson-Humphrey position on the war before the platform committee at the convention, was chosen as the Humphrey running mate. He made a good candidate and established himself as a national figure and a party leader. This status was enhanced by his address to a national television and radio audience as the spokesman of the Democratic party in the congressional election of 1970. He came close to becoming the titular head of the party, a role never accorded to Senator Humphrey after the defeat by Richard Nixon in the 1968 election. Muskie was also marked by the antiwar Democrats, a mark which was to hurt him seriously in the presidential campaign of 1972.

As Humphrey undoubtedly was hurt as a presidential candidate by his vice presidency, so was Muskie hurt by his vice presidential candidacy. There were political casualties on both sides of the Vietnam issue, Senator Morse and Senator Gruening, outspoken opponents of the war, were both defeated in the 1968 elections. Proponents of the war suffered, too, not in Senate elections, but as national candidates.

The Nixon administration followed.

The Nixon presidency was marked by contradictions; as was his campaign for the office. The methods he had used in campaigns for the House of Representatives and for the Senate were set aside. His campaign was restrained, almost antiwar. After his election, he continued the war with extended bombing and the "incursion" into Cambodia. But the Vietnam War did end during his administration. By report, he was displeased that Henry Kissinger, rather than he, Richard Nixon, was given the Nobel Peace Prize. I don't think either he or Henry deserved the prize, but between the two, Nixon deserved more credit for observing the end of the war than did Henry. I think it fair to say that, no matter to whom credit is given, quite possibly no one could have done any better in ending the war unless he had ended it sooner, but quite certainly no one could have done any worse.

The positive credits for Nixon as President were in areas in which one might have expected him to fail or not to have acted at all. Although his action in moving to have the Communist government of Vietnam recognized at the United Nations ran contrary to his position of opposition to that government—a position maintained throughout his entire congressional career—it was a commendable act. Nixon also deserves credit for the Salt I disarmament agreement, which was the first such agreement to set a limit on arms development and deployment, rather than to limit testing or define areas to be exempted from nuclear war.

His performance on domestic issues was similarly surprising. Whereas he might have been expected to be fiscally conservative (whether because of his desire to be reelected or because he was outbid by the Democratic Congresses with which he had to work), his record of fiscal responsibility was not good. This set up a situation that his successor Gerald Ford could not handle, nor, for that matter, could Ford's successor, Jimmy Carter.

Along the way, traces of the old Nixon showed through.

The most disturbing was not Watergate, but his "enemies list" of 1971. When completed, it included over two hundred persons, who were to be taken care of in various ways. The memorandum so disturbed William F. Buckley, Jr. that he wrote, "Dean's memorandum was an act of protofacism. It is altogether ruthless in its dismissal of human rights. It is fascist in its reliance on the state as the instrument of harassment. It is fascist in its automatic assumption that the state in all matters comes before the right of the individual. And it is fascist in tone: the stealth, the brutality, the self-righteousness. It is far and away the most hideous document to have come out of the Watergate investigation."

"Punishing one's enemies and rewarding one's friends" is an expression known to American politics. But "enemies" in this context usually has been a term applied to persons active in politics. Reward meant patronage—possible appointment to office, as postmasters, ambassadors, and the like. Punishment meant the denial of similar favors. All within the limits of accepted political practice. The Nixon list was quite different, both as to those included, and as to the means of punishment. First, it refined the political categories to include classifications such as "Black Congressmen." It also included many persons who were not directly involved in politics: journalists, businessmen, celebrities, academics, and whole organizations. More serious than the range of the lists were the methods proposed for dealing with the "enemies." The "fact of our incumbency"—that is, the occupancy of the White House and the control over executive agencies of government—was to be maximized. Attention was to be given as to "how we can use the available federal machinery to screw our political enemies." Grants and fed-

eral contracts might be denied. But there was also emphasis
on positive, affirmative action, by litigation and prosecution.
A separate briefing paper for H. R. Haldeman suggested how
the Internal Revenue Service could be made "politically responsive." As to Ed Guthman, an editor of the *Los Angeles
Times*—"It is time to give him the message." The advertising
firm of Doyle, Dane, Bernbach—"Should be hit hard starting with Dane." Ruth Picker and David Picker, of United
Artists Corporation, "should be programmed." Of Morton
Halperin of Common Cause, "A scandal would be most
helpful here." And so it ran.

The "plumbers" and Watergate followed almost inevitably. As certain of victory as any presidential candidate in
recent history, President Nixon and/or his campaign workers seemed afraid to go with an honest campaign and an
open one. Whereas "Watergate" had little bearing on the
outcome of the campaign of 1972, it led to the resignation
of President Nixon.

The press generally has taken deep bows for the coverage
of the Watergate case and for the resignation of Richard
Nixon. In fact the coverage of the case was almost an accident at its start, and afterward, an act of continuing perse-
verance of two minor reporters, Bob Woodward and Carl
Bernstein of the *Washington Post.* They were eventually sustained by the editor and publisher of their newspaper, rather
than by any broad press commitment. According to George
Gallup's poll, a month after the break-in at the Democratic
Headquarters, only half of the people of the United States
acknowledged having read or heard that the *Washington Post*
is to be credited for following the case.

The manner in which the Watergate case was pursued

raises serious questions of professionalism and ethics. It is interesting to compare the methods used by the "plumbers" of the Nixon campaign with those used by the investigative press, as reported in the Woodward and Bernstein book *All the President's Men.* The plumbers used illegal wiretaps; the press investigators had persons listen to telephone conversations on extension phones. The plumbers bugged their subjects; the investigative reporters eavesdropped and used confidential sources. The plumbers, or the administration, had the FBI check long distance phone calls with the telephone company; the investigative reporters persuaded sources in the telephone company to give them similar information. The plumbers and their principals were found guilty of obstructing justice; the investigative reporters narrowly escaped prosecution on the charge of tampering with a grand jury. The plumbers broke and entered; the investigative reporters used false identification or misrepresentation of their professional roles to get interviews. The plumbers rifled files; the investigative reporters examined, when not watched, what they could see on desks. The plumbers, at least some of them, demanded that they be paid off by the Nixon campaign committee; according to their book, the investigative reporters came close to blackmail by threatening to expose informants. The plumbers sought to justify their actions on the grounds that they were serving a high purpose, the reelection of Richard Nixon. The investigative reporters justified their methods on comparable grounds.

Richard Nixon did resign under threat of impeachment. He was succeeded by Gerald Ford, who pardoned Nixon and then ran a reasonably competent administration until his defeat by Jimmy Carter in 1976.

PART IV

ENTROPIC POLITICS

THE POLITICS OF THE UNITED STATES, and especially of the Democratic party, following Watergate and the end of the Nixon
administration might best be labeled "entropic," a state attributed to society generally, by Professor John Ahearn of
Stanford University, as having "no goal," and no "path of
effective action." "Entropy," said Ahearn, rules this uni-
verse. Of the multiple definitions of entropy, at least one can
be transferred with great relevance from the field of thermo-
dynamics and applied to the social and political order. That
definition identifies entropy as a measure of the "randomness, disorder, or chaos in a system."

This randomness is and has been manifest in this decade
—the last half of the seventies and the first half of the
eighties—in three major areas of public policy bearing on
the general good: economics and business, military and for-

eign policy, and politics and government. First it should be noted that we are the greatest consumers, even overconsumers, in the history of the world with the possible exceptions of the Ik, a mountain tribe in Africa who are reported to gorge themselves on a good day's kill without thought for other people or even for their own tomorrow, and the Romans, who provided the vomitorium as an adjunct to the dining room so that the banquet would be only temporarily interrupted.

An Environmental Protection Agency report published a few years ago noted that twenty-eight tons of materials from mines, fields, forests, and oceans are used each year per person in the United States—a measure of consumption twice that of the people of Western Europe, four times that of Eastern Europe, and one which cannot be realistically compared with consumption in countries in the backward areas of the world. Many countries of the world would live better on the waste of America, if it could be transported to them, than they do on their present supplies and resources.

We are overfed. One estimate has Americans on the average fifteen pounds overweight.

We are also overtransported and overfueled. Making up approximately five percent of the population of the world, we have about fifty percent of all the automobiles in the world—one car for every 9.8 persons. It is not the number of cars we have that is the serious consideration, but rather that our automobiles are oversized, generally overpowered, overly destructive, and wasteful. It is estimated that in the automobile culture of our country, estimated in dollars as slightly below $1 trillion, that some $150 billion is wasted each year. And we are overheated, overcooled, and overlighted, at least by relative standards; we consume one-third of the world's production of fuel.

We are certainly overdrugged, with both prescribed and over-the-counter drugs, overdoped, and poisoned by insect and weed killers, which we continue to use with social approval even though we suffer from overproduction of agricultural produce.

We are overadvertised, over-infotained (a new word coined by a CBS executive to describe television news, combining information and entertainment). Television news is not only given by local stations but to the nation in triplicate each evening by the three major networks. In addition, there is early news and late news, news updates, and promises of more news to come. There are bumpers and follow-ups, hints of generic news (say something about volcanoes) to come, and of specifics (say Mount Vesuvius or Mount St. Helens). About fifteen years ago, CBS went so far as to buy exclusive advance rights to film a prospective invasion of Haiti, the invasion to be financed in part by the advance payments for the television rights. ABC has for a number of years bought the exclusive rights to film the Indianapolis 500 auto race, including the right not to show the race until long after it has been run.

The new consumption, which goes with supply-side economics, has both passive and active aspects. Electric toothbrushes and electric can openers are on the market, along with electrically powered exercycles. Television sets have been manufactured which give a picture the instant they are turned on and with gadgets which allow the viewer to determine picture and channel selections by remote control. Powerboats have largely replaced rowboats and sailboats.

Snowmobiles have replaced sleds, skis, and snowshoes. Packaging has become a major industry, with paper and plastic wrappings cluttering streets of the cities and rural roadsides. Garbage disposal has become a major problem. Planned obsolescence is justified by both macro- and micro-economics. Cars, old before their time, go as the poet Philip Booth wrote "to Maine," or to North Carolina or West Virginia, or are crushed into cubes and sent to Japan. "No return" cans and bottles have replaced glass containers that could be returned and reused. Current waste and overconsumption would have Thorsten Veblen, were he still alive, blushing for shame at the modesty of his projection of "conspicuous consumption." We are hard-pressed to dispose of our trash, wastepaper, rubbers and plastics, nuclear waste—even former dictators.

We are overbureaucratized, yielding to magistrate proceedings, despite the warning of Jefferson and others that yielding would open the way to a loss of democratic freedom, and without seeming to realize or to care that there is in bureaucracy a danger that goes beyond that noted by de Tocqueville—beyond "the tyranny of the majority over minorities," to the ultimate democratic tyranny of the "majority over itself."

We are overincorporated. As early as 1831, James Kent, a legal scholar of the time, pointed out that the United States had made it too easy to organize corporations, noting that we had gone far beyond what was permitted under both the Roman and the English law. He saw danger in giving too much power to an institution of limited moral, social, and political responsibility.

Kent's warning has gone largely unheeded. In the years since 1831, a significant transfer of power to corporations has continued. This shift has been challenged only as far as the size of corporations. And it is challenged by liberals who do not seem to realize that the problem with corporations is not principally size, but substance, the nature of the corporation itself.

In the 150 years since Kent's warning, it is not only economic power that has shifted to corporate control. Although today approximately 80 percent of the economic and fiscal functions of the United States are directed through some form of corporate institution, many of them are given their corporate consciences, or souls, by the states of New Jersey and Delaware.

President Reagan and his administration have judged the growing power of the corporations to be a good thing. Congress, including liberal Democrats, have not been far behind him. Together they have given the corporation even more economic power through tax reductions, greater freedom to organize into larger and larger units, and relief from regulations and government direction.

Another major grant of power to the corporations was not initiated by Ronald Reagan, but was given over by liberals and reformers—groups such as Common Cause. The Federal Elections Act of 1975–76, strongly supported by Common Cause, permitted and encouraged the creation of corporation-controlled political action committees (PACs) whose organizational and management costs could be paid by the corporation with the use of money that otherwise might go to stockholders, to employees, or to society in the form of lower prices or taxes. The corporation PACs have become a major source of campaign funds, especially in congressional elections.

The third area in which there has been a tremendous

growth of corporate power is defense policy. President Eisenhower warned the nation of this danger in his farewell address in 1960, when he identified the existence of "the military-industrial complex," which had in fact been consolidated during his administration. Technology developed and controlled by corporations can conceivably define the national defense policy and dictate military strategy. A weapons system developed by a corporation in search of profits may well determine the fate of the nation.

Not just military policy, but its counterpart, foreign policy is increasingly subject to corporate influence. In the early decades of this century, corporations did exercise influence over foreign policy, but that influence could usually be identified and usually was in some degree subject to government direction, or at least coincided with government policy. Corporations were agents of the government. In some cases, in a kind of reciprocal arrangement, government became the agent of the corporation. Thus, United Fruit carried on trade and also executed national policy in Central and South America. The American sugar companies controlled trade in sugar and strongly influenced national policy toward Central American countries, especially Cuba, from the time of the Spanish-American War until Fidel Castro. Thomas Dooley was moved to write at the time of the Spanish-American War that if he were given a choice, he would rather be subject to a Spanish grandee than to an American vegetable, the sugar beet. The major oil companies directed oil and political policies, with less than complete success, for nearly half a century in the Middle East, and the copper companies were a major force in Chile.

The power of the multinational, or supranational corporations goes beyond that exercised by companies like United Fruit in earlier days, however. The multinational corporations are not agents, but have the attributes of sovereign countries. When President Reagan undertook to prevent Dresser Industries from selling high-technology pipeline equipment through its multinational connection to the builders of the gas line from Russia to Europe, he found that he was without power to intervene.

A fifth area in which further extension of corporate influence is being encouraged, through moral suasion and tax concessions, is that of culture—education, religion, and the arts. Corporations, by nature making judgments relative to the economic good of the corporation, may take the place in our culture of the patrons of the arts and education of earlier centuries, such as Italian princes, Dutch merchants, English landowners, robber barons. In keeping with this new development, Amway Corporation underwrote a European tour of the National Symphony Orchestra at the same time it was introducing its products and methods into Europe. Corporate control over the media is proceeding rapidly. More and more newspapers, radio stations, and television corporations are being taken over by public corporations, rather than being run by descendants of the past lords of the press, the McCormicks and Hearsts. Recent court decisions have given more freedom to corporations to generally use corporate money for political advertising and other forms of noncommercial communication.

We may be headed for a state of affairs similar to the schoolboy's definition of feudalism: a system in which everybody belonged to somebody, and everybody else belonged to the king.

In a recent settlement with its workers, General Motors, one of the more advanced feudal societies of our time, included the provision of legal aid services to its employees. We may anticipate that G.M. will soon establish its own courts, possibly with appeal to the courts of society in general, as in some cases of old when those subject to feudal courts might go to the king. Bowling jackets bearing the corporate seal have already replaced the livery of medieval times, and the next G.M. settlement may well provide for a G.M. common religion, a modern manifestation of the early principle that "the religion of the prince is the religion of the people."

Finally, we are overdefended, or better, "overdefensed," if we accept the estimates that we have sufficient nuclear weapon power to destroy the major population centers of the world several times, and to destroy the Russians that count at least twenty to thirty times over; if we accept that although we are better prepared to fight World War II than we were when we fought it, conventional wars and conventional weapons are obsolete; and if we acknowledge that guerrilla wars, principally helicopter wars, such as that which we carried on in Southeastern Asia, are unprofitable, unrealistic, and unwinnable.

We have passed through and discarded two major conceptions of nuclear security and superiority, and are now living by a third.

In the campaign of 1960, Democratic candidate John F. Kennedy charged that there was a missile gap between the Russians and the United States. "The gap" never quite achieved the status of a governing concept, especially when, after the election, the Democrats in power discovered that there was a "gap," but that it was in our favor. Maintaining or possibly widening the "gap" held as a rule for expanding defense procurement, until a more compelling concept was introduced sometime during the term of Robert McNamara as secretary of defense. That concept was described under the title of Mutual Assured Deterrence. In its early formulation, it was based on the declaration that if we could assure the Russians that we could destroy 20 percent of their population and/or 50 percent of their industrial capacity, that the possibility alone would deter them from an attack on us. Presumably, assurance that they could do the same to us would act as a comparable deterrence against any nuclear initiative war effort on our part.

When the arms buildup on both sides reached a point where each side had the potential to destroy the other beyond the 20 percent level, a new covering concept was introduced.

At the beginning of the decade of the sixties the words "strategy" and "strategic" carried traditional meanings; both applied to planning and actions. But by 1967 a change had taken place. In that year, the Johnson administration approached the Soviet Union with the possibility of holding talks on "Strategic Arms Limitations," not, as one might have expected on "the Strategy of Arms Limitations." What was introduced in the new testimony was a distinction between "strategic" weapons and "nonstrategic," or tactical, or just plain weapons. The weapon, in the new thought, had come to define its function.

By the early seventies, nuclear weapons thinkers had begun to talk about "strategic superiority" as a new measure of advantage. Even those who used the term had some difficulty explaining what it meant. Henry Kissinger, when asked what was meant by the term, responded by saying, "What in God's name is strategic superiority? What can you do with it?" Five years later, Kissinger said that he had spoken in a moment of pique in 1974 and that he did indeed know what constitutes "strategic superiority." He did not fully explain. It was left to the secretary of defense at the time, Harold Brown, who defined "meaningful strategic superiority" as a "disparity in strategic capability," which can be "translated into political effect."

Strategic superiority, reduced to quantitative terms, had come to be a measure of how many more Russians could we kill in a nuclear exchange, and, beyond that, how many more times could we kill the Russians—those that count— than they could kill Americans that count.

Melvin Laird, also a secretary of defense under Nixon, attempted a further explanation, when he said our goal in defense buildup was to match and exceed what we knew the enemy had; then, to match and exceed what they had the potential to produce; but to go beyond that, and match or exceed the momentum of their potential. This projection could carry one just short of infinity.

For some reason strategic superiority as a guiding principle faded as the decade of the eighties approached and a new measure of security was introduced: the percentage of gross national product that we were spending on defense relative to the percentage of gross national product the Russians were spending. The assertion was that we were spending a smaller percentage, and that, if we did not increase that percentage, a "window of peril" would be reached by 1985. We are spending well above 5 percent of our GNP on defense now.

Historians and philosophers of history through the centuries have noted two major general causes of decline: one, an unwise and destructive foreign policy, especially war, and two, internal fiscal and structural disorder. Both of these causes have run strongly against the Democratic party and against political, economic, and social order in the United States over the last three decades.

The war in Vietnam was a war with no clear goal and no "path to effective action." Both its purpose and its course of action were improvised. And as the costs of the war mounted, no responsible provisions were made—even in the Johnson administration—to spur the economic adjustments necessary to meet those costs.

The rate of inflation rose sharply from a base of 100 in 1967 to over 116 by the end of the Johnson administration. The Federal debt in the same period rose from $341 billion to $382 billion. The same trends were to continue during the Nixon administration but at accelerated rates. The index of inflation rose from the 116 level in the last year of the Johnson administration to 170 in 1976, the year in which Carter was elected, and the national debt increased from $382 billion to nearly $632 billion. Both measures of economic well-being and of success or failure of government fiscal policy were to get worse under President Carter.

During the Nixon administration the Vietnam War was continued largely under the same prescription of purpose and of methods applied during the Johnson administration. There were some changes in language but little change in the substance of the war, and no serious attempt on the part of either the President or the Democratic Congress to acknowledge the economic burden of the war. It was as though the war had been isolated, separated from continuing political judgment or response, while other issues such as that of nuclear arms or the recognition of China took center stage.

In those years, Congress—partly in self-defense, partly under the pressure of critics—was making its own contribution to chaotic government. Reform, reorganization, and restructuring of government and of politics, which were all advocated and supported in the name of efficiency, order, and higher morality, moved the country into a higher order of entropy. One clear example of harmful reform is the reinstatement of indexing, described as a bad idea whose time had come.

Indexing was in limited use in earlier decades, principally to determine farm price supports, but customarily the index of payments as provided by law was in the range of 75 to 85 percent of parity. An index also was used in setting minimum wages before the seventies. The major application in that decade was to social security payments, following a political contest in 1972 between President Nixon and the Democratic-controlled Congress, marked by veto threats and charges of misrepresentation, and ending in a 20 percent increase in social security payments. Evidently to protect itself from future pressures of the kind that had led to this increase, Congress went on automatic. Then, in the eighties, after a decade or more of talk of bracket-creep in income tax rates because of inflation, Congress (supported, if not led by President Reagan) moved to index tax rates in response to inflation, thus removing the one more or less automatic tax brake on inflation. It was a sure sign to the people that inflation was a reality.

New budget procedures were adopted in 1974 which, it was optimistically predicted, would resolve the issues of how much money the government might spend, how to spend it, and where the money was coming from. Authorizations, appropriations, and revenue raising were to be brought together in harmonious trinity. The results have been quite different from what was promised. Confusion has been the rule. The federal budget has increased. The federal deficits on an annual basis have grown larger. The national debt has reached new highs. Appropriations are sometimes approved in advance of authorizations, raising constitutional questions as to their legality. Delays in raising the debt ceiling have threatened to force the government to borrow money to meet current expenses. Continuing resolutions to keep the government going have become common. In its last act of desperation the Congress in 1985 passed the Gramm-Rudman Act, currently being challenged as to its constitutionality, and certainly subject to challenge as to its rationality, which proposes to assign to a government agency responsibility to reduce the expenditures already authorized by Congress and scheduled to be paid for. The House and the Senate have passed reorganization measures and adopted codes of ethics. The House has admitted television to its sessions. The Senate has done the same.

Increase in the number of roll calls has been encouraged by the introduction of electronic roll taking. In 1960 the House of Representatives had 180 roll call votes, that is 0.7 votes per working day. In 1970 there were 443, or 1.3 per working day. In 1980, following the reorganization and the introduction of new technology, there were 1,276 roll call votes, or 3.9 per working day. In the Senate a comparable proliferation of roll calls has occurred, the number increasing from 1.5 per working day in 1960 to 3 per day in 1980.

Senator Stevens of Alaska was moved to say that because of redundant roll calls, Congress "never finishes anything, never arrives at decision. Always," he said, "they are just preliminary decisions that will be addressed later. It's totally confusing to the public and even to ourselves." During the first Reagan administration, there were, by one count, thirty-six test votes on the MX missile in the House and in the Senate.

In 1981 the Senate voted twenty-five times on a budget reconciliation bill. In 1983 there were eight Senate roll call votes on the matter of what language to use in condemning the Soviets' shooting down of the Korean Air Lines flight 007. During a three-month period in 1983 the House of Representatives voted twenty-seven times on the nuclear freeze issue, including eleven votes in one week, and in a period of two days the Senate voted ten times on Senate salary and compensation proposals and then wiped out the ten votes by recommitting the proposal to a committee for further consideration.

A side effect of the rise in roll calls—one encouraged by press reporting—is the pressure on members of the House and Senate to have near-perfect attendance records on roll calls. A member who does not have such a record is generally labeled by the press as inattentive or failing in his duties, and almost certain to be assailed by a challenging candidate with questions such as "do you want a 75 percent congressman?" The worst manifestation of the roll call syndrome is the drive on the part of some members to have perfect attendance records. The precedent for this development was set by Senator Margaret Smith, who was the first member of Congress in modern time, possibly in all time, to achieve a perfect record on 1000 consecutive roll calls. Unfortunately, she was commended by the Senate for her achievement, her devotion to duty, and for other associated virtues. Other members both in the Senate and in the House have followed her example without any supporting evidence that their devotion to regularity has in any way served the Republic well.

What often happens is that a member who is absent on a day when ten or twelve roll calls are recorded will, upon returning, wait for a chance—say on an appropriations bill or a salary bill—to demand roll calls so that, since he cannot make up on the record the votes he has missed, he can build up his average. Then some other member who may have missed both of the masses of largely irrelevant roll calls will wait for a chance to build up his average by calling for unnecessary votes and roll calls in an almost geometric progression. In fact, attendance records in excess of 75 percent in the House of Representatives—if those included in the 75 percent are carefully selected as unimportant and irrelevant —and in excess of 60 percent in the Senate, applying the same standard, should be subject to criticism rather than to approval.

Congress did not restrict its action to internal reform but moved to general election reform in the aftermath of Watergate. The Federal Election Law amendments were passed in 1975, their purpose to eliminate corruption, the power of money, and to get better and wiser persons elected to national offices. These goals were to be achieved principally through two reforms: limitations on the amounts of money that could be contributed to and spent in campaigns, and government financing of federal elections. After adjustments in the law to meet a Supreme Court ruling as to the constitutionality of some of its provisions, the law went into effect in 1976. In the version of that year and in its current form, the law gives financial support directly only to presidential candidates.

Two presidents, Jimmy Carter and Ronald Reagan, have been elected with the help of the federal government funds. Congressional elections are not financed directly with federal funds, but those elections are subject to most provisions of the amended federal elections law. The cost of the campaigns, one of the evils cited by the advocates of the new laws, has gone up significantly since the passage of the reforms, principally because the laws legalized political action committees of corporations and unions, allowing both to use institutional funds to promote political action and to solicit campaign funds.

In a recent senatorial election in Minnesota, a state with a strong populist tradition, the Democratic candidate for the Senate spent between $10 and $15 million of his and his family's money, while his Republican opponent spent something over $4 million. The Republican won. Both the House and the Senate are getting more and more members whose principal income is unearned, in some cases from trusts set up not only by their fathers and mothers, but by grandfathers and grandmothers—even great-grandfathers and grandmothers (who evidently were not willing to trust their progeny with money even unto the third generation, possibly until the fourth generation, of biblical note).

Unless the election law is changed to allow larger contributions to candidates who are neither wealthy nor supported by corporate or labor groups, the prospect is that the number of the very rich in Congress will continue to grow. First sons who, thirty or forty years ago, would have been content to play polo or run the family business, or even lead a quiet life, now run for Congress. The names of members of Congress will begin to read like a list of *Fortune*'s Five Hundred. In recent years, Congress has had, or does have, a DuPont, a Heinz (of the 57 varieties), a Danforth of Purina Pig Chow and the Danforth Foundation, a Seiberling of tires, two Mortons of flour and salt, a Stuckey and a Brock of candy families, an Ottinger of plywood, a Reid of real estate and publishing, a Kennedy and a Taft of foundations, and others of lesser-known names, along with a sprinkling of former astronauts, quarterbacks, basketball stars, and at least one Olympic decathlon winner.

Along with reforms in the operation of Congress and of elections generally, the Democratic party proceeded through the seventies and into the eighties to reform its own procedures for selecting delegates to its conventions and for the conduct of conventions. The first major change was in the rules for the 1972 convention. The pressure for change came out of the acknowledged abuse of delegates at the Chicago convention in 1968, which led that convention to commit the party to set up a commission on rules changes. That commission was set up under the chairmanship of Senator George McGovern.

The 1972 rules proved to be just what were needed to assure the nomination of Senator McGovern, who applied them with the rigor of his Methodist ministerial background. While the unit rule for nonprimary states was outlawed, thus assuring McGovern his share of the delegates from the nonprimary states, the winner-take-all and other primary laws that discriminated against minority vote positions and candidates were not challenged. With 44 percent of the vote in the California primary, George received 100 percent of the California delegates. He also received all of the delegates from Oregon, Rhode Island, and South Dakota by applying the same rule.

Application of the new rules against secret-slate making and those requiring proper and proportional representation of minorities and of women (not a minority) led to the rejection of Mayor Richard Daley's Chicago delegation of fifty-nine people. They were replaced by a largely pro-McGovern delegation including blacks, Chicanos, and women, in proportion to their presence in the Chicago population.

Following the 1972 convention, the Democrats again moved to change the rules. In this effort, the principal target was the obvious discriminatory treatment of states with primaries in which the unit rule was allowed to apply and the treatment of states that did not have primaries and acted through nominating conventions. The chairman of the post-1972 Commission on Rules was Leonard Woodcock, president of the autoworkers union. One of the active commission members was Jimmy Carter.

Woodcock was subsequently the first major labor leader to endorse Carter for president. The rules adopted for the 1976 convention served the Carter presidential effort admirably. The new rules eliminated the winner-take-all primary. This meant that Carter was to receive in primary states his share of the delegates, according to his popular vote. Carter did marginally well in primary states, getting a good number of delegates that, under winner-take-all rules, he would not have received. In nonprimary states, especially in the South, he did not need a winner-take-all rule because he received nearly all of the votes. It is quite possible that without the rule change adopted in advance of the 1976 nominating process, Carter would not have been nominated, and Senator Muskie or possibly Senator Humphrey would have been. Certainly Carter would have had great difficulty securing the nomination.

After being nominated by the Democratic party in 1976, Jimmy Carter, asked for new authority and new procedures for picking his vice presidential running mate. The convention agreed, and the nominee returned to Plains, Georgia, with a more or less open permit to pick whomever he wanted for vice president.

The procedure for selection was an innovation in American politics. Substantively, what Carter did was to take applications for the office. A selected list of potential vice presidents was made up. Those included were asked to file application papers with the party nominee, to be followed by personal interviews. The list included Senator Frank Church, who had made a good run against Carter in a number of primaries, Senator Muskie of Maine, John Glenn of Ohio, Walter Mondale of Minnesota, Adlai Stevenson III, all qualified as potential vice presidents.

Essentially, what Jimmy Carter asked of the aspiring vice presidential candidates was information similar to what he had made public about himself. Primarily, this consisted of a medical report. He had published the facts that he was allergic to Swiss cheese (not American), hops, and beans. He also made public his financial status and his income tax returns, and asked his potential vice presidential candidates to do the same. He also asked each for a resumé. (The prospect of Senator Muskie submitting a resumé to Jimmy Carter was difficult for me to imagine.)

Mr. Carter made public much of his religious experience and beliefs. He told of having been reborn, and about his frequent daily prayers and communications with Jesus. He told of his sins, even of his occasional "lust in the heart."

In the choice of Senator Mondale, Mr. Carter made public at least one thing that impressed him. This was the senator's correction, or rather completion, of his medical report. In his first medical report to Mr. Carter, Senator Mondale had reported a condition of hypertension and the attendant medical treatment of that condition, as well as some related complications. Subsequently, according to Mr. Carter, the candidate for vice president had contacted him, asking whether he could amend the report and inform the presidential nominee that he, the vice presidential possibility, did have, in addition to hypertension, a hernia which was causing him no special trouble. In announcing this amendment, Mr. Carter said that he was much impressed by Mr. Mondale's integrity and thoroughness, since the disability now reported was one that might have gone undetected otherwise, possibly never discovered by the presidential candidate. Possibly he figured that a vice president caught between hypertension on the one hand and a hernia on the other would not be overactive or aggressive.

Jimmy Carter chose Walter Mondale as the party's candidate for vice president. It was a good choice; Mondale was an effective campaigner. His outstanding achievement was the victory, as it was acclaimed, over Senator Dole in the national television debate, a victory which may have been responsible for Carter's election.

It was into the confusion and contradictions of 1976 that the Carter presidency was born. More or less, by tradition, Republicans are expected in presidential campaigns to run against foreign policy, whether made at home or abroad, against the welfare mess wherever it is, and against governmental fiscal policy; Democrats are expected to run against unfair taxes, against concentration of economic power, and against unemployment. Whichever party is out of power usually charges that the country is either undefended, or if adequately defended, at unreasonable costs.

Jimmy Carter as a candidate exploited all seven issues. He said that U.S. foreign policy was being made in Washington instead of being made in the country; that taxes were unfair and that there was an undue and indefensible concentration of wealth in the country, thus voicing the accepted set of issues reserved for the Democrats. He did not stop there. He charged that there was a welfare mess in Washington, moving into an area usually restricted to Republicans, and then attacked the internal revenue code, one drawn up over the years principally by Democratic congresses, as a "disgrace to the human race," and finally challenged military policy, declaring that he was against the war in Vietnam, but only because it was run badly, hesitatingly, and without clear direction.

Carter ran against the Democratic record as much, if not more, than he ran against the Republicans.

For better or worse, and even when there was not much change, each administration from Truman's through that of Gerald Ford (short though it was) left some mark and memory.

Truman left the Marshall Plan, the commitment to NATO

and the United Nations, and the beginning of civil rights legislation. The stamp of his personality lived on. Some of his cabinet members continued as politically significant after their service in his administration ended. One or two are still in Washington.

Dwight Eisenhower left a pleasant glow and the covenants of John Foster Dulles, which later administrations accepted as obligations, legal and moral. Eisenhower also left the legacy of the military-industrial complex, which developed during his eight years in office, but which he warned of in his farewell address, one of his best. Some of his cabinet members carried on as public personages after Eisenhower.

The Kennedy administration left its mark in style, in continuing family involvement in politics, in the consequences of the invasion of Cuba and the missile crisis, and in other ways. Members of the Kennedy cabinet continued in the Johnson cabinet, and some continue today to be active in public service, as in the case of Robert McNamara, until recently head of the World Bank, Larry O'Brien as head of the National Basketball Association, and Dean Rusk as a teacher and lecturer on international law and foreign policy.

The Johnson administration made its historic mark in the escalation and pursuit of the Vietnam War, in the passage of major civil rights legislation, in its contribution to the dissolution of the Democratic party, and in the beautification of the city of Washington, principally through planting encouraged by Lady Bird.

The Nixon administration left the nation the heritage of Watergate, its flotsam and jetsam, the imprint of the Nixon personality, and the continuing presence of Henry Kissinger, among other persons and things.

The Ford administration, although transitional and short-lived, did leave a mark. President Ford is not forgotten, although his public appearances on golf courses and ski slopes get about the same amount of attention as do his political appearances or statements. The Helsinki Accords, approved during his administration, are a continuing force for judgment against Russia.

The Carter administration's passing was different from the others. It might be described as the "administration that never was." Certainly, it never took on an identifiable form, neither did it make a significant impression on U.S. domestic or foreign policy. The administration, in retrospect, appears as a vague of contradictions, of vacillation, of moralizing in a cloud of adverbs, with its ending lost in the return of the hostages in Iran in the middle of the inauguration of Ronald Reagan.

Many, I am sure, had hoped for a better departure for Jimmy Carter—at least somewhat like the Cheshire cat in *Alice in Wonderland*, leaving the remembrance of the smile, a sign of goodwill and openness.

It was not to be so. The ending came as shown in home video tapes released by the White House (one wonders why) showing the President getting ready to go to the inaugural ceremony, concerned, it appeared, about his need for a haircut, and asking that his handkerchief, his comb, his pocketknife, and cross be sent to him in the Oval Office.

Most of the members of his cabinet disappeared. The former secretary of state Cyrus Vance has surfaced in an article not on foreign policy, but on reforming the electoral reforms.

What was left, at least as it is being presented, comes close to Abraham Lincoln's description of a scene after a politician he knew had left as "floating about on the air, without heft or earthly substance, just like a lock of cat fur."

The Carter-controlled National Democratic Committee quite prudently foresaw that President Carter and Vice President Mondale might have difficulty in getting the party nomination in 1980 if the 1976 truly Democratic rules were left in force. The rules were changed in 1976 in the name of reform. Liberals—who were in the habit of supporting anything in the name of reform—supported the change. They seemed unaware that in order to be a successful peanut processor, as Carter had been, one must be able to "think small."

Although the new rules did not quite assure Carter's and Mondale's renomination, they gave them a clear advantage over challengers, especially if they had a number of challengers. Shortly before Senator Edward Kennedy announced his candidacy, a Carter and Mondale campaign spokesperson observed that because of the new rules and also because of the new provisions of federal law bearing on campaigns, Edward Kennedy's campaign would be much more difficult than the presidential campaigns of his brothers Jack and Bobby had been, principally because of the limitations of personal campaign expenditures and other legal restrictions.

Calculators rather than programs or noise-makers and paper hats were most important along the way to the renomination of Jimmy Carter in 1980.

The Democratic party which in 1952 had rejected Harry Truman as its candidate, after an administration of significant domestic accomplishments, the establishment of NATO, the initiation of the Marshall Plan, a beginning at advancing civil rights, and reasonable success in the Korean

War, in 1980 could not, or would not, replace Jimmy Carter, but ran with him to certain defeat with inflation at 13 percent a year and interest rates ranging as high as 16 to 20 percent. Carter was doomed to defeat by his own words spoken in the 1976 campaign, when he asserted that anyone who as president of the United States had allowed inflation and interest rates to reach the levels they had reached under the Ford administration should be disqualified as a presidential candidate. Defeat was further insured by the hostage-taking incident in Iran, by his loss of control over the weapons policy of the country, and by his failure to secure the passage of the SALT II arms limitation agreement.

The Reagan administration, which followed, defies historical judgment. The President seems to live in clearings, historical and intellectual, isolated, as though on separate movie sets, not only from current realities, but even from his own previous views. As long as there is sunlight in the clearings, why worry about the intervening jungle seems to be his attitude. The philosophy of the administration is largely a rerun of that of the twenties.

Despite the facts that Reagan has achieved no major foreign policy successes and that domestic reductions in the rate of inflation and interest rates have been offset by tremendous increase in the federal deficits and in the national debt, the defeat of the Democratic party's presidential and vice presidential candidates in the 1984 campaign came as close to total defeat as it is possible to come in American politics. Why?

Not content to go with the restrictive, incumbent-assuring rules of the 1980 campaign, Democratic party leaders, office holders, and officials of the labor movement moved to make the rules for convention delegate selection even more restrictive for 1984.

The whole procedure conforms to at least one of Parkinson's laws: institutions or persons in trouble try to insure survival, if not perpetuity, through procedural or legal support. The reality was that with the rules for the Democratic nomination for 1984, the party, although it had not regressed to the undemocratic procedures of 1968, had adopted rules that were more restrictive and more undemocratic—more clearly in violation of the principal "one person, one vote," and more centrally controlling than were the rules of 1968.

Vice President Walter Mondale was nominated as the party's candidate for president. In his campaign for the nomination, he asserted that he was "a real" Democrat—the purest Democrat of those candidates in serious contention, and that he was "ready." His claim to being a "real" Democrat was based on his having supported both the substantive and procedural positions of the party. His readiness came from his qualifications to represent the party in a campaign in which voters were being approached as potential clients. Mondale was "ready" to say, "Be my client. I will represent you." In this spirit he accepted late in 1983 the endorsement of the AFL-CIO and that of the National Education Association. He welcomed the endorsements, thanked both organizations for their support, and promised to represent them well. He later accepted similar endorsements from the National Organization for Women.

Less formally he offered to be the agent of Social Security recipients, farmers, minorities, the poor, the environmentalists, and others. He did this despite the fact that the interests of some groups among those from whom he sought support were in conflict with the interests of others.

Accepting the role of agent was consistent with the Vice President's professional and political background. He was, by professional training, understanding of the relationship between lawyer and client, which allows defense of causes and of persons in which or in whom one does not necessarily believe. Moreover, he entered politics when very young, not as principal but as a volunteer and a political operative. His first public office was by appointment as an assistant attorney general of the state of Minnesota. Subsequently, he was appointed attorney general following the resignation of the incumbent. In the first position he worked under the direction of the attorney general. In the second he was somewhat subject to the direction of the governor who appointed him. When his appointment term ran out he was easily elected to the office. This experience seemed to set a pattern for his future political actions.

In 1964, a Minnesota seat in the Senate became vacant when Hubert Humphrey became vice president. Mondale was appointed by then Governor Karl Rolvaag to succeed Humphrey. His principal rival for the appointment, Congressman John Blatnik, had been in the House of Representatives for eighteen years. The telling argument for the appointment of Mondale was that, if he was appointed, no block in the party would be irritated.

Mondale, without being chosen, made a tentative bid for the presidency in 1974. Discouraged by the response, he announced in November of that year that he was stopping his campaign, and that he would not be a candidate in 1976. Not only did he not run, but he supported none of the candidates, and when the Democratic convention was over, he was clear of any demerits for having challenged, questioned, or criticized Jimmy Carter.

He was chosen by Carter, in essence, appointed, as the vice presidential candidate—a procedure consistent with the method that had served Mondale well throughout his political career.

In 1984, although challenged in the primaries and, to some extent, in nonprimary states, he was, in effect, the appointed candidate of the labor movement, the party regulars, and party office holders.

Along the way, prospectively, Mondale had not left things to chance, but had been actively involved in changing party rules, so as to make more certain his nomination in 1984, and the earlier renomination in 1980 of the Carter-Mondale ticket, even when it seemed certain that that ticket was doomed to defeat.

Mondale was involved in developing and executing the move to reject the original Mississippi delegation at the Atlantic City convention in 1964 and, again, in the 1968 convention, when delegations from both Mississippi and Georgia were rejected and replaced. The Mondale interest in reform and accomplishing goals through rule changes and procedures was not limited to party rules. He was an active supporter of most of the reforms approved by the Senate in the seventies and advocated as vice president some that were not adopted.

In his campaign for the presidency, he spoke of his two significant contributions in the Senate: one, getting votes to change the filibuster rule, and two, actively supporting the effort to change the structure of the FBI after J. Edgar Hoover was dead. Both of these contributions had to do with procedure, or process, rather than substance.

Even as procedural changes both were questionable achievements. The filibuster rule, the old one, set up a classical conflict, something close to "trial by ordeal." A filibuster was not entered into lightly. Preparations required both mental and physical attention. It was under the traditional filibuster rule that the major civil rights legislation had been passed. The changes in that rule came after those major victories and did not eliminate filibusters, but provided that they could be carried on under complicated rules, which encouraged almost random filibusters, requiring neither the psychological or physical conditioning essential to filibustering under the old rule, but merely a mastery of Senate rules.

The filibuster had been a defensive procedure used primarily to prevent the passage of legislation. In the fifties and sixties, it was principally applied to civil rights legislation. The liberals had prevailed on most of those issues. The changes in the rules transformed the filibuster from its traditional function into a technical procedure, not so much of defense as of attack.

In comparable manner, the changing of the structure and function of the FBI was an action of questionable merit. The problems with the FBI under J. Edgar Hoover were not functional, but rather problems of persons—of the director, of attorneys general, of presidents. Under Hoover the bureau remained an agency; lines of responsibility were clear. Almost every action could be traced to an official, either the director, who was careful to define his authority, or to the attorney general, who had ordered the actions taken by the director, or to the president. The changes effected by Congress after the death of Hoover transformed what had been an agency into a bureau in which the lines of responsibility were blurred and accountability made more difficult. Evidence of the change was clear when the director of the agency was asked to explain the procedure by which members of Congress were set up for the ABSCAM project. He reported that he had not ordered the action, nor had been directed to conduct it, but that he had known about it, and that it had just come up through the agency. This is a clear demonstration in practice of Hannah Arendt's exposition of pure bureaucracy in which no one is responsible.

Again, Mondale, in describing how President Carter and he had given new meaning to the vice presidency and had institutionalized that office, gave his response to a presidential request for suggestions for reforming the elective process. He recommended the extension of federal financing of elections to congressional elections. He recommended the abolishing of the electoral college and the direct election of the president by popular vote. He also recommended the easing of requirements and procedures for voter registration. All his suggestions dealt with procedure rather than substance.

The Mondale procedure in selecting his vice presidential running mate followed the 1976 Carter method, but was more thorough and comprehensive.

The search began, according to report, early in the spring, well in advance of the convention. A preliminary list of fifteen or twenty names was drawn up and staff members assigned to begin to gather information about each of those listed. The sorting out of possible candidates began with invitations to visit the Mondale Minnesota home, in North Oaks, a suburb of Minneapolis and St. Paul.

The first to be called, but not chosen, was Tom Bradley, a black, who had been mayor of Los Angeles and who had just lost in a bid for the governorship of California. Lloyd Bentsen, senator from Texas, with strong southern support, followed, as did Dianne Feinstein, the mayor of San Francisco. Mayor Feinstein is Jewish. Others on the Mondale list were Mayor Wilson Goode of Philadelphia, Henry Cisneros, the thirty-seven-year-old Mexican-American mayor of San Antonio, Martha Layne Collins, governor of Kentucky, and Geraldine Ferraro, Italian and a member of the House of Representatives. Others, reportedly, were not called to North Oaks but reached by telephone and told they were under consideration, most notably, a Greek, Governor Mike Dukakis.

The choice was Geraldine Ferraro.

Geraldine Ferraro's personal problems may have hurt the Democratic ticket marginally. Walter Mondale's television image and protection fell short of Ronald Reagan's. But the defeat stemmed from more than personalities and accidents of politics. It was substantive and integral, a defeat of the party. This contrasts with the McGovern defeat in 1972, in which McGovern ran with support from those looked upon as party irregulars and newcomers, not party leaders and the labor movement.

The Democratic party after the defeat of Mondale and Ferraro was left without a spokesperson (such as it had in Adlai Stevenson after each of his defeats by Eisenhower). And it was left without a platform such as it had in the

Kennedy campaign of 1960, following eight years of the Eisenhower administration.

At least a half-dozen foundations, and institutes, some set up by potential presidential candidates, have been established to find out what the Democratic party is or what it should be. Individual Democrats struggle to establish what kind of Democrat, or liberal, they are—traditional, unreconstructed, reconstructed, sane, neo-, et cetera. One study group recommends a return to the past, another a great leap forward. One potential presidential candidate sees the future of economic development around the "Pacific Rim." Another looks to new technology—to mining asteroids and gathering nodules of rare materials from the bottom of the sea. While the search for policy and progress goes on, national needs are present and obvious. Unemployment hovers at 7 percent. Housing needs are not being adequately met, the agricultural industry, at least a large part of it, is in deep trouble. The number of persons living in poverty continues to increase. Major medical needs of the country go unmet. The military buildup continues. Family life is disintegrating under various pressures, or in transition, needing attention. The balance of trade is highly unfavorable, the national debt rising close to $2 trillion and projected to reach $3 trillion by the close of Reagan's second term. An ill-directed military buildup continues. The nation's space program appears to be in a state of serious disorder. The most popular investment in the world is not oil, but investment in claims against future tax collections in the United States.

Democrats seem separated from reality, overwhelmed by general statistical measures, the gross national product, interest rates and inflation rates—lower than they were in the

Carter administration, but higher than they were in earlier Democratic administrations—and by the continuing apparent popularity of President Reagan and his administration.

The ship of state may be losing its way and settling slowly in the water, but the deck appears to be level and there is no water in the first class cabins. While the Democrats flounder in distractions, their opposition is finding even deeper, ideological satisfaction in other developments spawned in the shadow of deficit and debt. A major social good, as they see it, is that under pressure of the budget deficits and mounting debt, welfare and other domestic programs are being cut back. They find satisfaction in other developments not so directly related to the deficit-debt reality. These bear directly on a continuing move to give advantages to the capital factor of production. Capital, or those who control it and profit from it, has a growing advantage over the labor factor.

Unemployment is at a level at which labor analysts say management or capital can effectively control wages and worker benefits. The trend of wages, in recent years, has been downward. In 1977 average weekly wages of private nonagricultural workers in the United States was $189 a week. Measured in the value of 1977 dollars, those weekly wages fell to a little over $171 per week in 1985, a decline of $17 a week.

Downward economic pressure on U.S. labor is further intensified by the importation of foreign labor, legal and illegal, and of raw materials and manufactured goods, produced by low-wage workers in countries like Taiwan, Korea, and China. A recent news program showed steelworkers in India, who were earning one dollar a day, producing manhole covers for Baltimore, Maryland, a city suffering decay as a major steel-producing center.

Goods are also coming in from countries such as Germany and Japan, which have a built-in indirect subsidy in that their costs do not include the magnitude of taxes paid by American workers and industry for defense, much of which is committed to the protection of those countries.

The pressure on American labor is further increased by competition from automated machinery, developed, built, put in place with the aid of investment credits, tax exempt industrial bonds, and other subsidies from governments, federal, state, and local.

Those who control capital, also have a current advantage over the second of the traditional factors of production, namely, land or natural resources. Agricultural prices are generally depressed. In the United States, farm prices, set against prices with 1977 as the low-index base, are at an index number of 79. The prices of most industrial minerals, iron ore and copper, for example, are depressed. Oil is now under severe downward pressure.

Perhaps more important, within the capital system itself, special, integral advantages have been given and are being given to capital and income on it. Capital gains have been progressively given a preferred position, as contrasted with other forms of income, to the point that capital gain, at least for tax purposes, has a status bordering on that of the sacred monies of the temples of ancient times.

The changes in the amount and the percentage of income taxes collected from corporations as compared to that collected from individuals gives a rough indication of what has happened and is happening. In 1950, approximately $25 billion of taxes was collected through income taxes: $15 billion from personal income and $10 billion from corporate income, a ratio of 3 to 2. In 1960, the total tax collected from the two sources was just over $60 billion, $40 billion from individuals and $21 billion from corporations. The ratio had become 2 to 1. By 1970, the amount collected was slightly over $120 billion of which $90 billion was levied on individuals and $32 billion on corporations. The ratio was almost 3 to 1. In 1980, $244 billion was collected in individual income taxes and $64 billion-plus from corporations, a ratio approaching 4 to 1. It is estimated that in 1986 individuals will pay over $356 billion in income taxes and corporations about $68 billion, a ratio falling between 5 to 1 and 6 to 1.

Capital gains get special treatment in rates, in holding period, and in sequestration. Pressure continues for further reduction of corporate income tax rates and for the continuation and extension of special exemptions and special treatment of corporate income through depletion allowances, depreciation, investment credit, and retention of earnings. Dividends and interest income are given partial exemption from income taxes and protected in trusts and foundations, as well as in corporate financial structures.

Capital is developing its own theological and philosophical support. Established religions find that they can accommodate capitalism to their theological and moral doctrines. Fundamentalist preachers are moved to take their religious-economic beliefs into politics.

A large, more or less permanent, national debt will not in its effects run contrary to the trend toward concentration of control over capital, and its special treatment. In fact, the transfer of control over capital will be significantly enhanced by the increase of the national debt. If, as is anticipated, the total national debt by 1995 will be close to $4 trillion, about three-fourths of it will be held by individuals of some wealth, foreigners and Americans, by financial institutions, and by corporations. The other one-fourth will be held by government agencies and by state and local governments and their agencies. The annual cost of servicing the three-fourths of the debt in nongovernmental control will come close to $300 billion a year. The federal government will then be, as it is now in lesser measure, the instrument through which taxes, largely levied on wages and salaries, will be collected, transferred, and, more than that, transformed into capital, capital gains, and other tax-privileged forms of income. The federal government thus will contribute to the increased and continuing concentration of wealth, of power over wealth, and of production of wealth.

Perhaps most reprehensible is our failure to recognize or to admit that our relationship to the rest of the world is not that of a nation with clearly defined sovereign power such as it was in the twenty years following the end of World War II, when our power—economic, military, and even ideological—went unchallenged in the non-Communist world. A combination of forces and developments, some beyond and some within our possible control, have made us, in fact, a colony of the world.

Neocolonialism is marked, like classical or traditional colonialism, by several salient features. The first is increased investment leading to control of the colonial economy from outside. In the case of the United States, control is exercised not by an imperial mother country, but increasingly by a number of foreign countries, entering a relatively free investment field. With investment comes control.

For example, the U.S. government's efforts to prevent the export of U.S. technology, such as forbidding the sale of advanced computers to France (when France was suspected of intending to use the computers to help build a nuclear bomb), might well be undercut or circumvented if the technology could be exported under the protection or immunity of a multinational corporation with direct investments in U.S. companies. It should be noted that to some extent the United States does restrict direct foreign investments in minerals, communications, air transport, nuclear energy, and inland shipping activities, although foreigners are generally permitted to purchase noncontrolling interests in voting stock, even in companies operating in these restricted fields. During the 1950s and 1960s, the U.S. government did intervene to discourage the building of automobile and tire factories in Russia on the grounds that Soviet military potential might be advanced by such facilities.

The importance and danger of foreign control over U.S. economic interests was made clear by the president of a major oil company during the oil embargo of 1973. He reported that his company had, in fact, allocated a larger share of the company's foreign oil production to the United States during the embargo than would have been warranted on the basis of each country's share of business before the embargo. Had he not been an American, or had his company not been controlled by Americans, it might have been much more difficult for him to have made the decision favoring the United States.

A second characteristic of colonialism that is beginning to

mark U.S. trade relationships is our growing role as a supplier of raw materials and a purchaser of manufactured goods. The British established and maintained such a trade relationship during the colonial period of United States history, and it was one of the grievances that led to the American Revolution. Today, however, we ship timber to Japan and import fiberboard; we ship scrap metal to Japan and import automobiles; we ship coal to Germany and import petrochemicals.

A third characteristic of colonial status is the absence of full control over the domestic monetary system. For a variety of reasons, the United States has lost full control over its money—witness inflation and a highly unfavorable balance of payments. Formal acknowledgment of this took place during the Nixon administration when the dollar was devalued and allowed to float, subject to the pressures of the international money markets. Dollar instability might be even worse if other countries did not have large dollar holdings and therefore an economic interest in stability.

But the neocolonial status of the United States is also evident in noneconomic areas. For instance, U.S. military forces are now expected to defend other nations. In fact, in some cases the United States is under contract by treaty to defend other countries, notably West Germany and Japan. And, within the last three decades, without clear contract or treaty obligation, our military forces have defended the South Koreans and the South Vietnamese. Under the Eisenhower Doctrine, they are committed to respond to requests from governments that believe themselves threatened by Communist takeover. The role of U.S. troops in these instances is comparable to that of colonial mercenaries, although in this instance the countries calling on the colonial troops do not even pay the costs, except marginally in the case of West Germany and Japan.

Under these conditions, our military policies can be imposed from outside. This is a clear historical example of what Charles de Gaulle defined as a state of dependency or colonialism. De Gaulle's point was that a first-class nation should never allow a foreign policy or military policy to be imposed upon it, and that when foreign policy or foreign commitment (in de Gaulle's case it was French involvement in Algeria) begins to weaken a nation either physically or morally, that foreign policy has to be rejected.

A second noneconomic sign of neocolonialism is our growing loss of control over our own borders and over immigration. The great influx of people from Puerto Rico in the 1950s was wholly within the terms of treaty agreements. Nevertheless, that influx was disorderly and disruptive and accompanied by many social problems, especially in New York. The more recent and continuing serious problem involves illegal immigration from South and Central American countries, especially from Mexico. This immigration does not have the legal support of treaty agreement. Estimates of the number of illegal immigrants from these countries reach as high as one million persons a year. The failure to control illegal immigration from Mexico is defended by some on the grounds that strict enforcement of immigration laws, more vigorous and thorough patrol of the border, harsher penalties, and quick deportation would "provoke" Mexico and lead to unrest among Mexican-Americans already in the United States. Possibly such actions would be provocative, but such a possibility does not eliminate the reality of the movement of immigrants into the United States, without legal right, either by statute or by treaty.

More recently there has been an influx of refugees and expellees from Cuba, along with an increase in the number of illegal immigrants from other Caribbean and South American countries. The shipping to colonies of criminals and other undesirables, such as those whom Castro has been accused of sending to the United States, has a strong precedent in the British colonial practice of sending criminals to Georgia and later to Australia.

A more subtle manifestation of neocolonialism is the challenge to the status of the English language in the United States. There has been both a practical and a legal submission to demands that at least some parts of the country should become bilingual or multilingual.

Imperial nations traditionally impose their languages—or try to do so—as did the Portuguese in Brazil, the Spanish in South America, the British and the French in their African possessions, and in less successful efforts, the British with the Boers in South Africa.

The process is more subtle in the United States. It is being done in the name of civil rights, of good citizenship, and of economic and cultural equality. Yet it runs contrary to historical evidence of the dangers of bilingualism in a country, and contrary to the warnings of anthropologists like Margaret Mead, who has written:

Bilingualism, and especially bilingualism developed in some compensatory effort to absorb immigrants, increase social mobility, equalize inequalities, as a step toward openness and membership in the world, can be a trap. It becomes, as so many analyses of past and recent experiments in relationships between majority and minority languages have shown, a worse trap if there is no literacy in the mother tongue . . . But once it is recognized that it is the potential antagonism of all dualism and all polarization that is harmful, the next step is easy to take and has some of the delightful simplicity that all good educational innovations have. Simply introduce a third language.

(*Teacher's College Record,* May 1978.)

Her obvious conclusion is that a two-language system is unstable, divisive, and should be avoided unless we are prepared to move toward a multilingual society.

This new relationship of the United States to the rest of the world may be, in some measure, the inevitable result of changes in international economics, in communication, and in new politics. But the changes have wrought a powerful transformation in the role of America in the world, and the role of politics within America. The realities should be recognized, and the limits of power in major areas—economic, political, and military—weighed as our politicians go forward to make U.S. policy.

The state of the Republic, although existing in a different historical context, substantively would be similar to that described as marking the Roman Republic in Sallust's observation in the first century B.C. Roman civilization, he noted, was then marked by unequal distribution of wealth, depopulation of the countryside, exorbitant veterans' demands, high unemployment of citizens, the widespread use of slave labor, bread and circuses for the poor, debt-ridden farmers, costly military ventures, oppressive taxes levied on some, and a government controlled by wealth, unprepared to comprehend the magnitude of the state or its innumerable problems.

For Democrats or Republicans, for all who are concerned about the good of the Republic, there is no need to search for issues, but to choose among issues that are clearly evident, that can and should be made the subject matter of political action.

The choices and the determination of action will have to be made principally in this decade by persons left over from the "apathetic fifties," by persons now well over thirty, who in the sixties, warned against the judgments of anyone over that age, by those carried forward as "yuppies" or "Yumpies" from the seventies, a decade that never achieved clear identification or label. Concern and commitment cannot be manifested as openly and dramatically as it was in the sixties. It is clearly easier to demonstrate and stir opposition against a real war than to stir it up against a potential one or against an arms program. There are clearer reasons for active support of making civil rights legislation than for "enforcement," for new laws and court decisions than for "affirmative action." It is expecting much, if not too much, to look for support of causes, when spokesmen and leaders for those causes are in disagreement, or confusion.

Yet I sense a deep and continuing concern among this responsible generation, not just with the direction and substance of their own lives, in professions and occupations, but a concern, also, with the bearing of their personal and private lives on society—a concern about professional and community ethics, about social justice, patriotism, and the good of the commonwealth.

There are ten or more major issues of high moral, social, and political significance that demand attention from this generation:

The most serious of these issues is unemployment. With interruptions—primarily resulting from wars (Korea and Vietnam) and high inflation in the Carter administration, which caused the rate of unemployment to fall—the rate of unemployment has been rising progressively since the decade of the fifties and is currently holding at an official rate of about 7 percent, between seven and eight million persons.

The current level of unemployment is intolerable. "Paper fixes" and explanations by economists neglect the real problem. To provide millions of American workers, including new entrants into the work force, with useful and lasting jobs, Congress should encourage the redistribution of work. Work can be redistributed either by shortening the work year, or workweek, or workday, whichever is more appropriate for the industry or business. If the workweek were shortened from forty hours to thirty-five hours for 24 million workers (about a quarter of the work force), then the private sector could offer jobs to three million unemployed workers. In addition, if overtime were disallowed, another one million jobless workers could be employed. In a short period, the unemployment rate could be reduced to less than 5 percent.

Since the adoption of the forty-hour/fifty-two week "standard" work schedule in the 1930s, there have been over forty years of historic advances in labor and business technology. With these advances and the spread of automation, the "standard" work schedule has become outdated and must be revised. The results of the distribution of work are not necessarily limited to the elimination of unemployment. Other economic good could follow, in the way of increased productivity and a drive toward greater consumption by those who are now underconsumers.

We need today the confidence and wisdom demonstrated by Henry Ford in 1914 when he instituted the five-dollar/day minimum wage and the eight-hour workday and when in 1926 he became the first U.S. manufacturer to adopt the five-day, forty-hour week. In answer to his critics, Ford said, "The country is ready for the five-day week. It is bound to come to all industry. The short week is bound to come because without it, the country will not be able to absorb its production and stay prosperous." In answer to his critics who suggested that more leisure for workers would mean more drunkenness and wasted time, Ford predicted accurately that "the people will become more and more expert in the effective use of leisure." And he added, "It is the influence of leisure on consumption which makes the short day and the short week so necessary. The people who consume the bulk of goods are the people who make them." "People," he said, "with a five-day week will consume more goods than people with a six-day week." And, we can assume, work harder, so as to produce or have access to goods to be used in leisure time. The Russians have not learned this lesson. Their problem with alcoholism is, by report, much more serious than is ours with a five-day week.

And then there is the issue of agriculture. The United States needs a new approach to multinational trade in agricultural products. Congress must reassure foreign buyers that this country will not resort to another embargo. Food should not be used as an instrument for foreign policy. Humanitarian consideration aside, food embargoes are shortsighted policies with severe, long-term costs for American farmers.

To restore our credibility as a farm exporter and to expand the markets for U.S. agricultural products, Congress should establish an International Agricultural Agency (IAA), comparable to the Canadian Wheat Board. The IAA should be an independent agency that is free from the kind of political domination and intervention which obstructed grain sales to the Soviet Union during the Johnson administration, and prohibited grain sales to the Soviet Union during the Carter administration.

As for trade, since 1945 the United States has pursued a policy of relatively unrestricted trade. We tolerated, because of our economic strength, some discriminatory practices on the part of other nations. We acknowledged no limits to the potential of our economy to absorb imported goods. In short stretches, the balance of payments might run against us, but not in the long run. Not so today. The unfavorable balance of payments is now a serious problem. The merchandise trade deficit of 1985 rose to over $124 billion. Tariffs and quotas imposed by the United States invite retaliation by affected countries. But one inequity affecting international trade—the disproportionate share of defense costs for the non-Communist nations, borne directly by U.S. taxpayers and indirectly by the U.S. economy—is beyond challenge.

A defense import tax should be imposed on U.S. imports bought from any country protected by treaty arrangements with the United States like Japan and West Germany. The amount of this duty should be equal to the difference between the percentage of the Gross National Product (GNP) devoted to defense by the United States and by the exporting country selling goods to our domestic importers. On average, the tax assessed on relevant imports would be roughly 3 percent of the value of the imported goods.

The defense import tax will enable our allies to contribute more to their own defense, while eliminating the unfair trade advantage enjoyed by these nations at the expense of U.S. taxpayers and domestic manufacturers and their workers.

Housing. Many Americans, especially young families and low-income families, are being kept from buying their own homes by the high cost of housing, or are being obligated to spend a disproportionate share of their income on housing. Congress should amend the home interest deduction policy to provide relief and help for home buyers and, at the same time, eliminate or reduce a tax advantage of some magnitude for persons of wealth in the tax deduction allowed on home mortgages.

In the past, Congress has given special consideration, under the tax and banking laws, to the private institutions concentrating on home finance. This Federal support was justified on both social and moral grounds. Under the home interest deduction policy, many people invested in their homes with the knowledge that their returns would be less than if they invested their savings elsewhere, but with the confidence that their investment was more secure and served a social purpose. Inflation has undermined this "compact." Congress can help restore it.

The basic home interest deduction should be maintained, but allowed only against tax rates in the average bracket. With this reform, wealthy taxpayers would be limited in the amount of home interest deduction they could claim. At the same time, the common practice of borrowing on home mortgages to use money to invest in other commercial ventures would be discouraged. Consequently, the amount of money available for home mortgages would increase.

Second, a new interest deduction should be created to encourage even greater savings to finance new homes. In this case, taxpayers who have paid off their mortgage to less than fifty percent of the value of their home (including those who have repaid this debt entirely), should be allowed a tax deduction on the interest earned from the investments in home mortgage financing institutions for investments totaling no more than fifty percent of their home mortgage. Such a deduction will help to build a larger pool of funds for home mortgages and will also serve as a hedge against rising property taxes for people eligible for this new interest deduction. Savings and loan associations should get back to home financing.

Responsible political participants should stop playing the rate making game relative to the tax on earned income, the tax on wages and salaries, and look to the taxation or lack of taxation of the other two classically defined factors of production and sources of income, namely, land (i.e., minerals and other real resources) and capital.

They—or we—should not shrink from consumer taxes designed to discourage wasteful, socially undesirable consumption, not just of cigarettes and liquor, but overconsumption of more serious social consequences, such as that manifest in oversized, overpowered, and overfueled automobiles. The waste within the automobile culture has within it the possibility of savings of as much as $200 billion a year, according to some estimates.

The burden of payment of the enormous national debt, much of it incurred for current questionable defense expenditures, is being extended not to fall on the next generation, but on the one beyond that. If the expenditures were for a past war which extended security and safety to that generation, the imposition of the burden of payment, or of a part of that payment, would be justified. This, however, is not the case.

Taxation to hold the line, if not reduce the debt, should be imposed principally on those persons and institutions that have benefited most from excessive government expenditure and inflation. Accumulated capital, identified and unidentified, should be the principal target of tax gatherers. One Wall Street expert set the value of corporations, not reflected in the stock market figures, as approaching $500 billion. CBS is an example. It was represented as being worth about $3 billion, until Ted Turner offered $6 billion. Getty Oil was considered to be worth $3 billion when Pennzoil made its offer, $6 billion when Texaco made its offer, and nearly $11 billion by a Texas court.

The power of corporations must be curbed and directed for that power now threatens the public good in business, finance, and in broader areas of culture. The corporation is not a person with full moral and social responsibilities. It is a legal construct. It is what has been made with limited liability.

Because of its limitations, its moral and social deficiencies, the corporation must be constantly watched and judged by its performance. Corporate power should be limited and redirected.

Corporate employees should be assured greater freedom to move or change jobs without sacrificing economic security. To reduce their dependence on a particular corporation, workers need sound unemployment compensation that is not discontinued or seriously diminished in value if a worker leaves a corporation or if the corporation leaves the worker.

Corporations must be made to abide by the law. All laws, particularly those prohibiting price fixing, internal corporate manipulating, exploitation of workers (including migrants and illegal aliens), pollution and false advertising should be strictly enforced.

Corporations must assume greater social responsibilities in the economic areas, by providing more employment, job training, and environmental protection in return for the limited legal liability and favorable tax rates they have been given. The privileged position of feudal lords must be denied them.

The power of corporations, arising from their growing contributions to educational and cultural institutions and programs should be carefully limited.

The political power of corporations, through the Political Action Committees, allowed under the Federal Elections Act of 1975–76, should be curbed, if it cannot be wholly denied to them.

Those concerned about political and personal freedoms should take the initiative in challenging bureaucracy, espe-

cleateanletBarBasedBasBasBasBasBasBasBasBasBasBasBasBasBasBasBasBasBasBasBasBasBasBasBasBasBasBasBasBasBasBasBasBasBasBasBasBasBasBasBasBasBasBasBasBasBasBasBasBasBasBasBasBasBasBasBasBasBasBasBasBasBasBasBasBasBasBasBasBasBasBasBasBasBasBasBasBasBasBasBasBasBasBasBasBasBasBasBasBasالبBas

cially those with power over the basic liberties of the American people. I cite three in need of special attention, not one of which has been of any special concern to the Reagan administration:

First, the Federal Elections Commission, established by the Federal Elections Law of 1975–76, exercises near-arbitrary power over the electoral process and administers a law which encroaches on almost every guarantee in the Bill of Rights and in other provisions of the Constitution, including due process, separation of powers, and equal protection of the law. This commission should be abolished through repeal of the 1975–76 law, or, if that is not possible, the commission should have its bureaucratic powers carefully limited and defined.

Second, the Federal Communications Commission, which has the potential for dangerous control over news, education, culture, and politics. The best way to proceed without threatening freedom of speech is widespread ownership of radio and television stations, rather than the consolidation now being approved. Multiple station ownership should be challenged, the networks broken up, and ownership of TV and radio stations by newspapers should be severely limited.

And third, the Internal Revenue Service, which has the power to interfere, by interpretation and action with minimal Constitutional restraints, in almost every facet of our citizens' lives—economic, family, cultural, political, and even religious—should not be exempted from the Constitution, and its agents should be made personally responsible for violation of Constitutional protections of privacy, due process, and of the law, in the way which in recent years members of the FBI have been held responsible.

When tax law is such that it cannot be enforced within the limits of the Constitution, the law should be changed.

Finally, responsible political participants should challenge absolutely the concepts and historical judgments now used to justify militancy and the arms buildup. The premises and the language of self-declared authorities must be challenged. The distinction between "strategic" and "tactical" nuclear weapons must be denied. Overriding concepts such as Mutual Assured Destruction must be repudiated unless their sponsors can give proof of validity. Wholly relative standards for estimating military strength such as percentage of Gross National Product being spent on defense must be rejected.

The idea that history, or national military policy is a continuum—from administration to administration, from Madison to Reagan—which cannot be interrupted by rational decision, must be repudiated.

And, as a philosophy of government, we should attempt to define the direction and limits of affirmative action, unless we are prepared to accept "equality" of all kinds as a guiding objective, thereby proving the accuracy of de Tocqueville's warning of this inherent danger in a democracy.

These times do not quite deserve, by historical standards, to be called "times that try men's souls." They certainly are times that try persons' minds. They are times that call for a general demonstration of "public happiness," which John Adams defined as a willingness on the part of the colonists to take up public responsibility, to make common decisions, and to follow those decisions. It was, said Adams, a disposition so strong among the colonists that the Revolution was bound to succeed.

The "pursuit of happiness," our inalienable right according to Jefferson and the Declaration of Independence, includes our responsible citizens' attention to "public happiness" as well.

INDEX

Marx, Karl, 42
Marzitelli, Frank, 6
Mead, Margaret, 246–47
Medicaid, 167, 168
Medical research: funds for,
    19–20
Medicare, 167
"Meet the Press" (television
    program), 157, 158
Metcalf, Lee, 48
Mexico, 245
Meyer, Agnes, 141
Meyner, Robert, 134
Middle East, 112, 212
Military-industrial complex, 29,
    129, 212, 228. *See also* Army
    Corps of Engineers
Miller, William E., 165
Millikin, Eugene, 53
Mills, Wilbur, 30, 32, 33
Minimum wage, 132
Minnesota: postwar politics in,
    4–10
Minnesota State Fair Board, 42
Mississippi River projects, 26–28
Mitchell, John, 154
Mondale, Walter, 225, 226,
    231–37
Monroe Doctrine, x, 127
Monroney, A. S. Mike, 123, 124,
    138
Moore, Margaret, 9
More, Thomas, 102, 103
Morse, Wayne, 56, 74, 96–99,
    140, 175, 183, 184, 199
Mossadegh, Mohammed, 128

Mounier, Emanuel, 38
Moynihan, Daniel Patrick, 116
Mulligan, Joseph, 183
Multinational corporations,
    212–13, 243
Murray, George, 41
Murray, Phil, 7
Muskie, Edmund, 58, 61–63, 155,
    170, 199, 225–26
Mutual Assured Destruction,
    257
Mutual Assured Deterrence, 215

N

Nasser, Gamal, 127
National Council of Churches,
    178
National debt, 27–28, 217–19,
    231, 238, 241–42, 253
National Institute of Health, 19
Nationalist China. *See* Taiwan
National Organization for
    Women, 232
National Teachers Organization,
    232
NATO, 111, 118, 127, 227, 230
Neighborhood Youth Corps,
    168
Nelson, Gaylord, 40
Neocolonialism: America as
    victim of, 242–47
New Deal, 167–68
New Yorker, 192
New York Post, 188
New York Times, 152, 189, 194

Raftery, Antoine, 103
Rankin, John, 13, 24–25
Rayburn, Sam: beliefs of, 11–14;
    customs associated with, 31,
    33, 34, 48; mentioned, xi, 17,
    134, 139, 161
Raye, Martha, 180
Reader's Digest, 166
Reagan, Ronald, 117, 130, 211,
    213, 222, 229, 237. See also
    Reagan administration
Reagan administration, x, 27, 32,
    218, 220, 231, 238, 239
Reorganization Act of 1945, 12
Resolutions: use of, by
    presidents, 112–13, 128
Reuther, Walter, 134, 159
Riggs, Robert, 144
Robertson, Willis, 69
Rockefeller, Jay, 135
Rockefeller, Nelson, 86–87
Roll calls: congressional, 219–21
Rolvaag, Karl, 233
Rooney, John, 16, 18, 20–21
Roosevelt, Eleanor, 124
Roosevelt, Franklin Delano, 32,
    71, 85, 86, 129
Roosevelt, Franklin, Jr., 136
Rosen, Milton, 6
Rostow, Walt, 110
Rovere, Richard, 192
Rowe, Jim, 163
Ruby, Jack, 152
Rusk, Dean, 149, 154, 170, 172,
    173, 177, 181–82, 228
Russel, Mrs. Jasper, 9–10

Russell, Richard, 53, 55, 58, 82,
    152–53
Russia, 128–29, 181, 214–15, 220,
    229, 251

S

Sabath, Adolph, 33–34
St. John's College, 42, 144,
    165
St. Lawrence Seaway, 26
St. Thomas College, 4–5, 8
Salinger, Pierre, 193–94
Sallust, 247
SALT treaties, 200, 215, 231
Scali, John, 116
Scharper, Philip, 183
Schlesinger, Arthur, Jr., 189,
    192
Schmitt, Mike, 8
Scranton, William, 116
SEATO, 127
Senate: McCarthy's experiences
    in, 53–103
Senate Finance Committee, 61,
    64, 80, 146
Senate Foreign Relations
    Committee: under Truman,
    111; hearings on Vietnam
    War, 169–75, 179, 184;
    mentioned, 146
Senate Public Works Committee,
    66–67
Seniority: in the Senate, 53–54,
    63
Shatzkin, Mike, 194

T

Truth in Packaging Act, 100
Turner, Ted, 254

U

U-2 flights: and CIA, 128
Unemployment, 239, 249
United Auto Workers Union, 9
United Fruit Company, 212,
213
United Nations, 114–18, 200,
228
United Nations Charter, 114–16
United States: as colony of the
world, 242–47
United States Constitution: 22nd
Amendment, 85–86; 25th
Amendment, 86–88, 130

V

Vance, Cyrus, 229
Vandenberg, Arthur, 53, 111–12
Vatican: McCarthy's diplomatic
mission to, 144–45
Vaughan, Harry, 79
Veblen, Thorsten, 210
Veterans bills, 13–15
Vice-Presidents: selection of,
154–63, 225–26, 236–37
Vietnam: UN recognition of,
200
"Vietnam Conflict: The Substance
and the Shadow" (the
Mansfield report) 170–72,
174

Vietnam War: and Eisenhower,
126–27; and CIA, 128; and
JFK, 149; and LBJ, 149, 158,
167, 169–88, 228; effects of,
on US economy, 217; and
Carter, 227; mentioned, 61,
74–75, 91, 102, 249. *See also*
Anti-war movement; "Kill
ratios"
Vinson, Carl, 30
VISTA, 168
Voting rights, 59, 65, 100
Voting Rights Act of 1965,
100

W

Wallace, Henry, 109
Wallace, Lew, 166
"War Powers Act," 85
Warren, Earl, 152
Warren Commission, 151–53
Washington Post, 43, 141,
202
Washington Symphony Orchestra,
213
Watergate affair, 97, 201, 221,
228
Watkins, Vernon, 99
Weaver, Robert, 185
Wechsler, James, 188
Weir, Roy, 36–37
West Germany, 240, 244–45,
252
Westmoreland, William, 179–80
Wiggins, Russell, 115